Analytics Best Practices

A Business-driven Playbook
for Creating Value through Data Analytics

Prashanth H Southekal, PhD, MBA

Technics Publications

Published by:

2 Lindsley Road, Basking Ridge, NJ 07920 USA
https://www.TechnicsPub.com

Edited by Riaz Howey
Cover design by Lorena Molinari

All rights reserved. No part of this book may be reproduced or transmitted in any form or by any means, electronic or mechanical, including photocopying, recording or by any information storage and retrieval system, without written permission from the publisher, except for brief quotations in a review.

The author and publisher have taken care in the preparation of this book but make no expressed or implied warranty of any kind and assume no responsibility for errors or omissions. No liability is assumed for incidental or consequential damages in connection with or arising out of the use of the information or programs contained herein.

All trade and product names are trademarks, registered trademarks, or service marks of their respective companies, and are the property of their respective holders and should be treated as such.

First Printing 2020

Copyright © 2020 by Prashanth H Southekal

ISBN, print ed.	9781634628273
ISBN, Kindle ed.	9781634628280
ISBN, ePub ed.	9781634628297
ISBN, PDF ed.	9781634628303

Library of Congress Control Number: 2020935686

Endorsements

"Dr. Southekal proves why he is one of the leading thinkers on data and analytics today. 'Analytics Best Practices' is an indispensable guide for business leaders and those looking to get into the analytics field on the nuances, challenges, and immense opportunities with data. His well-researched, technology-agnostic, example-laden book includes sage advice on everything from how to value data, how to formulate hypotheses, how to engineer disparate data sources, how to deal with a variety of data quality issues, and perhaps most importantly, how to create a data-driven culture."

Douglas B. Laney
Principal, Data & Analytics Strategy Caserta
Author of "Infonomics"
United States

"Dr. Southekal's latest book starts with the accurate premise that most organizations are data rich but insight poor. It is written for enterprise data architects but contains insights that are useful for anyone with an interest in developing and improving competence in data analytics. What I like about this book is its focus on real-world best practices with an extensive set of practical tips and tricks. It provides an important bridge between the data management and business operations sides of a business. My favorite best practice is how to communicate insights through data storytelling and change management."

Professor Michael Wade
Cisco Chair in Digital Business Transformation
Professor of Innovation and Strategy, IMD Business School
Switzerland

"Prashanth did it again! His second book starts with the right title – it is always about BUSINESS VALUE. Data and Analytics leaders are appointed to increase value or drive lower costs. The practices explored here will help anyone interested to achieve these goals."

Mario Faria, Gartner Research Board, United States

"Dr. Southekal's book is a treasure trove of best practices and practical examples from the field of Data Analytics. From Stakeholder Objectives to Change Management, Data Compliance to Advanced Analytics, this book covers it all with concise and great examples. One can see years of Dr. Southekal's deep passion and expertise in this field shining through the pages of this book. Anyone who cares deeply about driving benefit from becoming data-driven would benefit tremendously from reading this book."

Upen Varanasi
CEO and Co-Founder, Riversand Technologies Inc, United States

"Leading companies are investing heavily in data and analytics initiatives, yet results remain elusive – 98.8% of firms report active investments in data and analytics, while less than half (46.7%) report that they are competing on data and analytics. Why the gap between investment and outcomes? Dr. Prashanth Southekal has created a practical guidebook for realizing business value from data and analytics investments. Highly recommended."

Randy Bean
Founder and CEO, NewVantage Partners
Contributing author for Forbes and Harvard Business Review,
United States

"Prashanth gives practical, concrete guidance to design your data and analytics program that will drive your business goals. He addresses the necessary technology, process, and organizational dimensions. He also touches on important and current topics such as compliance and monetization. It's a great book to read and then to keep as a reference."

Andrew Sohn
Partner, NewVantage Consulting, United States

"Prashanth's book is accessible and practical – an excellent guide for corporate leaders who want to produce meaningful business results from the use of data and analytics written in an easy-to-digest style that aims to create true business value as opposed to an academic collection of best practices. For those with an only basic understanding of data and insights, the book will layer the knowledge, as best practices build on each other in order of increasing complexity. After reading the book, novices can confidently ask the right analytical questions to start conversations about the value and competitive advantage of data. For seasoned business people with some data and analytics successes under their belts, the book will provide a structured guide for repeatable and sustainable development of value-generating analytics."

Irina Pelphrey
Senior Director, Merchandising Operations, Walmart
United States

"Another piece of gem from Dr. Prashanth Southekal! I thoroughly enjoyed reading the book. I have reviewed and read many books in the market about data analytics. Unlike those books that jump straight into focusing on implementing analytics strategies solutions coupled with technologies that support it, what is unique about this book is that it covers the end to end lifecycle of data asset (and analytics is just one component of the many components of data lifecycle) that is critical if you want your organization to be truly data-driven enabled by having the right data culture. This book takes a very balanced and practical approach and provides guidance on how to create sustainable business value out of data and analytics initiatives.

This book is a must on the desks of business executives and decision-makers at all levels in an organization who want to truly understand what it takes to become a successful data-driven organization with the right data culture to create measurable and sustainable business value/impact out of their data asset."

Ram Kumar
Executive Head and Senior Vice President, Quantium, India

"Prashanth not only delivers the art of the data possible, but he also explains the science behind it. Deriving actionable insights from data requires that linkage to be clear between art and science, and this book does just that."

Chris Leonard
Director, Strategy and Digital Transformation, Plains Midstream
Canada

"Dr. Southekal presented the book at our Institute (SPJIMR), and this was attended by several colleagues, including myself. The coverage of topics was fabulous. His style is lucid, meaningful, and very purposeful. He connects the framework with real-life examples, and that makes eminent sense for all practitioners.

I strongly endorse reading the book to all professionals who want to learn or apply analytics in their businesses for better outcomes."

Dr. Hemant Manuj
Associate Professor and Area Head – Finance
S.P. Jain Institute of Management and Research (SPJIMR), India

"Leveraging business value from data analytics is a challenge for many organizations today. The *Analytics Best Practices* book from Dr. Prashanth Southekal provides pragmatic guidance and techniques based on industry best practices and supported with real-world examples. It is one of the most comprehensive and well-researched books I have come across on data analytics. It presents the ten best analytics practices in the entire analytics value chain and the data lifecycle with the practical, innovative, and realistic capabilities to implement them. I highly recommend this book for anyone looking to realize the full potential of data and analytics as it links the data strategy with tactics."

Ameet Shetty
Former Chief Data and Analytics Officer, McDonald's Corporation and SunTrust Bank, United States

"Prashanth's book simplifies the complex world of data analytics and allows data engineers, business analysts, and leaders alike to understand the drivers of bringing valued results to an organization. Whether you are new to the world of analytics or are an experienced data professional, this book provides the tools and tips to build a successful analytics program, project, and model. It helps build a foundation for the new and great reminders for the skilled. This book will help drive better results for you and your organization!"

Matthew Joyce
Senior Solution Architect
SAS-Institute, Canada

"Data and analytics outcomes are still widely undervalued, even with many organizations operating data teams yielding robust analytic processing. Dr. Southekal's latest book breaks down how to effectively leverage insights from the data to harness robust economic value and thus competitive differentiation to your organization. I would encourage all professionals to read this easy to navigate, thoughtful, and pragmatic book as it is relevant to all of us seeking to maximize the ROI for our organizations."

Lisa M. Wardlaw
Former EVP, Global Chief Digital Strategy & Transformation Officer, MunichRe
United States

"Payload was in a position of having large amounts of latent data which Dr. Southekal was able to transform into revenue-generating products that add value to both Payload and its customers. Using Dr. Southekal's approach described in his book, we have not only created high-value data products for existing users but also opened a new side to our business previously not considered. This has, in turn, opened new opportunities both in data and the application itself, giving us a holistic insight into our industry and how to tie all corners together to the benefit of all our customers, new and old alike. The power of Dr. Southekal's books is in their pragmatic value to any organization seeking to gain competitive advantage and take both themselves and their customers to the next level."

Chris Lambert
Chief Technology Officer (CTO), Payload Technologies
Canada

"In a well-written fashion, Dr. Southekal portraits the key elements for best practice analytics in this book. In a pragmatic way, he provides the reader with a comprehensive understanding of the many different aspects of analytics. Aspects ranging from defining the most basics like 'what is analytics and what is not' to comprehensive descriptions of what to consider in the process from data collection to analytics insight generation. Anyone looking for a practical guide to build an analytics foundation would benefit greatly from reading this book."

Jesper Hybholt Sorensen
Co-Founder, Finance Analytics Institute

"In this book, Prashanth has thoughtfully distilled his 20 years of experience as a skillful practitioner in data analytics. You will find an intelligent narrative within the chapters highlighted with supportive evidence by relevant references and quantitative proof. Prashanth guides you through his comprehensive perspective in order to craft a meticulous strategy for accurately applying data science principles to achieve maximal impact throughout business architectures. This book should occupy a frequently used shelf for any data scientist or organization who wants to get the most out of their data."

Lexington Blood
Venture Partner, 7BC.VC
United States

Acknowledgments

This book reflects over two decades of my analytics and technology consulting, research, and teaching experience. There are many people who have positively impacted this book writing project. Writing this book was a unique learning and collaborative experience, and it has been one of my best "investments" to date. During the entire book writing project, I had the privilege of having discussions with top analytics researchers and industry experts who were instrumental in giving a better shape to this book.

First and foremost, I thank Dr. Gahl Berkooz, Vice President of Data, Analytics, and Monetization at ZF Group for writing the foreword for the book. Before joining the ZF group, Dr. Berkooz was head of Global Data Insights and Analytics at Ford Motor Company and was the Chief of Analytics, Global Connected Consumer Experience, with General Motors. Dr. Berkooz is acutely aware of how important data analytics is to the company's ability to thrive in the global marketplace. I would also like to express my sincere gratitude to Steve Hoberman of Technics Publications for publishing this book.

Special thanks to Santosh Raju, Lance Calleberg, Fergle D'Aubeterre, and Pavana Damle for taking the time to peer-review the book and giving valuable feedback. Also, some of the best analytics practices were validated by industry experts and from a large group of industry professionals who provided their perspectives on the articles I posted in LinkedIn and DataScienceCentral. In a line, analytics professionals from Australia to India to the UK to US/Canada have contributed directly or indirectly to this book.

I am extremely grateful to my former employers, clients, and my students at IE Business School (Spain), University of Calgary (Canada) and S.P. Jain Institute of Management and Research (SPJIMR) (India) for providing me opportunities to learn and understand the nuances of managing data analytics initiatives. Finally, writing a book while running my own IT advisory company DBP-Institute (DBP stands for Data for Business Performance) included many hours away from my family. It took me about two years to write this book. My wife Shruthi and my two wonderful kids Pranathi and Prathik understood how important this book is for me and to the analytics community and bestowed me with terrific support.

Prashanth H Southekal, PhD, MBA
Calgary, Canada
April 2020

Contents

Foreword _____ 1

Introduction _____ 3

Chapter 1: Data Analytics and Competitive Advantage _____ 5
    Analytics, intuition, and data _____ 7
    About business data _____ 12
    Data and competitive advantage _____ 15
    Data in the balance sheet _____ 19
    About analytics best practices _____ 22
    Conclusion _____ 25
    References _____ 25

Chapter 2: Best Practice #1 - Tie Stakeholders' Goals to Questions and KPIs _____ 27
    Why is this a best practice? _____ 30
    Realizing the best practice _____ 32
    Conclusion _____ 41
    References _____ 41

Chapter 3: Best Practice #2 - Build the High Performing Analytics Team _____ 43
    Why is this a best practice? _____ 43
    Realizing the best practice _____ 45
    Conclusion _____ 52
    References _____ 53

Chapter 4: Best Practice #3 - Understand the Data from the Analytics View _____ 55
    Why is this a best practice? _____ 65
    Realizing the best practice _____ 66
    Conclusion _____ 73
    References _____ 74

Chapter 5: Best Practice #4 - Source Data for Analytics Strategically _____ 75
    Why is this a best practice? _____ 80
    Realizing the best practice _____ 81
    Conclusion _____ 89
    References _____ 90

Chapter 6: Best Practice #5 - Make Data Compliance an Integral Part _____ 91
    Why is this a best practice? _____ 92
    Realizing the best practice _____ 95
    Conclusion _____ 100
    References _____ 100

Chapter 7: Best Practice #6 - Focus on Descriptive Analytics for Data Literacy _____ 101
    Why is this a best practice? _____ 104
    Realizing the best practice _____ 107
    Conclusion _____ 114
    References _____ 114

Chapter 8: Best Practice #7 - Use Continuous Refinement and Validation _____ 115
    Why is this a best practice? _____ 118
    Realizing the best practice _____ 119
    Conclusion _____ 124
    References _____ 124

Chapter 9: best Practice #8 - Leverage Analytics for Data Monetization _____ 125
    Why is this a best practice? _____ 126
    Realizing the best practice _____ 128
    Conclusion _____ 135
    References _____ 136

Chapter 10: Best Practice #9 - Support Analytics with Enterprise DG _____ 137
    Why is this a best practice? _____ 138
    Realizing the best practice _____ 139
    Conclusion _____ 143
    References _____ 144

Chapter 11: Best Practice #10 - Implement Insights with Data Storytelling _____ 145
    Why is this a best practice? _____ 147
    Realizing the best practice _____ 149
    Conclusion _____ 154
    References _____ 154

Chapter 12: Conclusion _____ 157
    Case study: Data insight product for Payload Technologies _____ 160
    About bad analytics _____ 168
    Selecting statistical tools for analytics _____ 171
    Closing thoughts _____ 172
    Reference _____ 173

Appendix 1: Data Quality Dimensions _____ 175
Appendix 2: Analytics Abbreviations and Acronyms _____ 177
Appendix 3: Analytics Glossary _____ 181

Index _____ 191

Foreword

I met Dr. Southekal through Mario Faria, who leads Gartner's program for Chief Data Officers. Ours are unprecedented times for the application of science to advancing the practice of business, and Data and Analytics are at the forefront of this transformation, neigh, revolution. Starting my career as an entrepreneur and company founder, later a management consultant, and now a corporate executive, I was delighted to have been introduced to Dr. Southekal and his project, as it provided an enjoyable retrospective on some memorable projects.

The book you are holding in your hands contains wisdom and advice that any analytics practitioner would benefit from. For the neophyte, it will serve as a source of ideas on how to progress their mastery of the métier, and for the experienced practitioner, it is a good reminder of solid practices that withstand the test of time. In the paragraphs below, I share how the best-practices Dr. Southekal exposes in this volume played out in some projects from the past (these appear in quotation marks).

I have personally deployed many, if not all, the best-practices eloquently elucidated by Dr. Southekal. When I served as Chief of Analytics for General Motors' Global Connected Consumer Experience Division (Onstar), we developed and deployed General Motors' first Big Data Customer Analytics Data Set and used it to create personalized incentives with advanced analytics models. This project was complex and required significant investment and attention, ultimately affecting dealership operations. We had to, as Dr. Southekal puts it, "Tie stakeholders' goals to questions & KPIs." To make this system sustainable, we had to "Support analytics with data governance" and extensively "Implement insights with data storytelling and change management."

At Ford, I had the privilege to "Build the high performing team for analytics." In the Information Management and Analytics area, we went from two people in 2005 to over a hundred in 2014. We pioneered data governance at Ford. Building a team that is willing to constructively disrupt with data and analytics is important for the success of any analytics function. At Ford, I also had the opportunity to establish "Make data compliance an integral part of analytics." That is an arduous task, and possible only when the approach is "Source data strategically." Our work at Ford resulted in a monetization value of close to $2 billion and received praise in Sloan Management Review.

At Acorns, a millennial-oriented Fintech Startup, I had the opportunity to mentor the team to create a highly personalized user experience using Data and Advanced Analytics. This was an excellent example of "Leverage embedded analytics and data products for data monetization" and refining the models and approach with "Use continuous refinement and validation as the mainstay of advanced analytics."

Last by not least, as a Data and Analytics leader, you, the reader, are an educator and advocate. Data literacy and showing that you understand the data in the business context are most important to gain the confidence of your business and to be able to bridge the gap between those who understand the business and those facile with Data and Analytics methods. This is the focus of the practices "Focus on descriptive analytics for data literacy" and "Understand the data from the analytics point-of-view."

In summary, I hope you enjoy this volume and the insights so diligently collected by Dr. Southekal. As described above, they all have a place in "the real world."

Gahl Berkooz, Ph.D.
Vice President of Data, Analytics, and Monetization, ZF Group
Greater Detroit Area, MI, United States

Introduction

Today, data is considered the world's most valuable resource. According to Eric Schmidt, former CEO of Google, the amount of data created in less than two days is equivalent to the volume of data created from the dawn of civilization to 2003! Faced with overwhelming amounts of data, organizations across the world are looking at ways to derive insights from data analytics and make good business decisions for better business results. However, not many organizations are successful in transforming their data into insights. In January of 2019, research advisory firm Gartner reported that 80% of analytics insights did not deliver business outcomes. So how can a business enterprise avoid analytics failure and deliver business results?

This book – ***Analytics Best Practices: A Business-driven Playbook for Creating Value through Data Analytics*** will improve the odds of delivering enterprise data analytics solutions successfully. This book is a sequel to my first book – *Data for Business Performance*, where the focus was more on data management. This book is for anyone who has a stake and interest in deriving insights from data analytics and focuses on three key differentiating "what is in it for the reader" aspects.

- **Practicality.** This book offers ten key analytics best practices for successfully delivering analytics initiatives for your organization. The objective is to offer prescriptive, superior, and practical guidance to the readers. The focus is on tactics.

- **Completeness.** Data analytics is more than data science or statistics. This book looks at data analytics best practices holistically across the four key data analytics domains i.e., data management, data engineering, data science, and data visualization.

- **Neutrality.** This book is technologically agnostic and will look at the analytics concepts without any reference to commercial analytics products and technologies. A business leader or a team or an organization that is keen to derive insights from data can use this book regardless of the IT products or analytics ecosystems deployed in the company.

This book has 12 chapters. The first chapter will provide a quick introduction to data analytics and the role of data and analytics in delivering improved business performance. The next ten chapters will discuss each of the ten best analytics practices from a tactical perspective. The last chapter, chapter 12, will discuss a case study where these analytics best practices were implemented along with other analytics topics like bad analytics and key statistical tools. All chapters have tips in the side note to further bolster your success in the analytics implementation. To support these twelve core chapters, Appendix 1 is on the 12 data quality dimensions, Appendix 2 has the list of analytics abbreviations and acronyms, and Appendix 3 contains the analytics glossary.

To get the best out of this book, I recommend you reading the 12 chapters sequentially. There are some overlapping topics that will be partially discussed in one chapter and covered in more detail in later chapter(s). Also, there is a dependency on each of the chapters to the preceding chapter. Directly going to the middle of a chapter might not give you the necessary background and context.

I hope you will find my book useful. Happy reading! Be data savvy!

Prashanth H Southekal, PhD, MBA
Calgary, Canada

CHAPTER 1

Data Analytics and Competitive Advantage

"In God we trust; others must bring data."

Edward Deming

Today, data is a key resource for improving business performance for enhanced insights, operations, and compliance. It is not only the data-driven companies such as Facebook, Google, Uber, Netflix, and Amazon, but also companies like Domino's Pizza, Goodlife Fitness, Lego, John Deere, Novartis, and many more that are leveraging data and technology for better business performance and results. Lloyd Blankfein, CEO of Goldman Sachs, an American multinational financial services company, stated "We are a data and technology firm" [Brittany, 2018]. While data and insights have long considered valuable even from the time when French emperor Napoleon Bonaparte said "War is 90% Information" in the 18th century, three key developments have spurred recent interest in data and analytics:

- **Data Capture.** Technological advances on sensor technology based on IoT (Internet of Things), e-commerce, social media, mobile devices, and personal electronic devices have propelled the business to capture incredible amounts of data at a very low cost.

- **Data Storage.** The explosion in data storage capabilities such as better computing hardware and cloud computing have enabled businesses to store large amounts of data reliably than ever before

- **Data Processing.** Advances in telecommunications networks and computational approaches have helped companies to effectively access and process massive amounts of data quickly and efficiently.

Such is the impact of data and technology that data today has replaced oil as the world's most valuable resource. In 2018, an average American spent 6.3 hours a day on digital media – creating and consuming content [Brynjolfsson and Collis, 2019]. According to Eric Schmidt, former CEO of Google, "the amount of data we create in less than two days is equivalent to the volume of data created from the dawn of civilization to 2003!" [Siegler, 2010]. Faced with overwhelming amounts of data, business enterprises from Retail to Financial services to Energy sectors across the globe are looking at ways to derive insights from data analytics and make good business decisions. The global market intelligence firm International Data Corporation (IDC) estimates the spending on data and analytics to reach US$ 274.3 billion by 2022 [Haller and Satell, 2020]. However, not many organizations are successful in transforming their data into insights.

- Moore's Law: Computational power doubles every 18 months
- Kryder's Law: Storage capacity doubles every 12 months
- Metcalfe's Law: Value of a network grows by the square of the size (nodes) of the network

In January of 2019, Andrew White of the research advisory firm Gartner reported that 80% of analytics insights did not deliver business outcomes [White, 2019]. Mckinsey consulting says, fewer than 20% of the companies have maximized the potential and achieved analytics at scale [Miranda, 2018]. So how can a business enterprise avoid the analytics failure and deliver results? This book will discuss the ten key best practices for successful data analytics. But before discussing those best practice chapters, this chapter will outline key reasons for the importance of data analytics in business.

Analytics, intuition, and data

There are many definitions of enterprise data analytics. One of the reasons for so many definitions of analytics is mainly because software vendors define analytics based on the products they sell. When SAP says analytics, it is an umbrella term that covers enterprise resource planning (ERP), data warehousing, business intelligence, enterprise performance management (EPM), master data management (MDM), governance, risk, and compliance (GRC). When SAS-Institute uses analytics, it is mostly predictive analytics, prescriptive analytics, and machine learning (ML). For Tableau, analytics is mainly dashboards. This has created varied definitions for analytics, and today analytics is a catch-all term from any activities from data capture to statistical analysis to data visualization. However, at the fundamental level, **analytics is using data for gaining insights by asking the right questions.**

No Questions + No Data = No Analytics

There are three main types of analytics that provide business insights. They are:

1. Descriptive Analytics, which is using historical data to ask: "What has happened?"
2. Predictive Analytics uses statistical models to ask: "What could or will happen?"
3. Prescriptive Analytics uses optimization techniques to ask: "What should we do?" or "What will make it happen?" Basically, prescriptive analytics recommends the best solution relative to a set of criteria or constraints.

These three types of analytics are shown in Figure 1.1; an illustration adapted from the work of the research advisory firm - Gartner. However, analytics is not a linear process; more complexity and effort always doesn't always lead to higher business value or better analytics maturity.

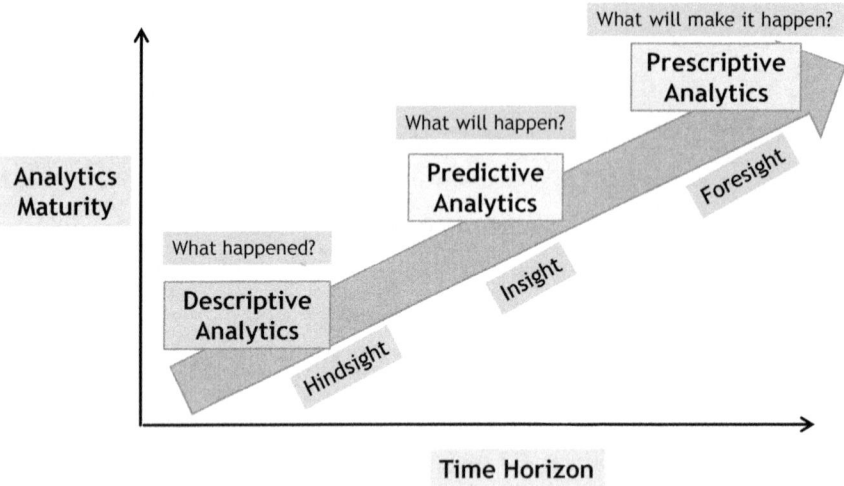

Figure 1.1: Three types of data analytics

Analytics is not a deterministic process. It is an evolutionary process where the insight needs of the businesses constantly change, the organizational capabilities continuously mature, the data sets grow and sometimes even degrade, and the technological capabilities to process the data improve over time. Working in analytics projects often is like shooting a moving target. As a simple example, if one is looking for one single value for the average price of crude oil between 2015 to 2018, it could represent mean, median, mode, weighted average, and more. While all these values are factual and correct, each of the above metrics gives a different crude oil price value, and each value is subject to varied assumptions and conditions. As a metaphor, analytics is like a compass that has some degree of ambiguity and subjectivity; it is not like a GPS (Global Positioning System), which is precise and accurate.

While the primary purpose of analytics is to gain insights using data, insights can also be derived from intuition – the ability to understand or know something based on feelings rather than facts or data. Human beings are naturally irrational, and irrationality has defined much of human life [Ariely, 2010]. In a survey by *The Economist* in 2014, 73% of respondents said they trust their intuition over data when it comes to decision-making [Olavsrud, 2014]. This begs the question of when human intuition is used and when data should be used for getting insights. Intuition is typically relied upon in the following situations.

- When time is too scarce to collect data, analyze it, and derive insights. Personnel in the firefighting, ICU (intensive care unit), and police services typically do not have much time available for deriving data-driven insights. In this scenario, the solution is to quickly respond to the situation.

- When there are well established or a restricted range of actions, for example, when a car has a flat tire, the intuitive decision is to change the tire. The normal course of action when you are thirsty is to drink water. You don't need data to make these obvious decisions as there are no choices. Again, insights and actions depend on the questions. If the question was, what made the tire go flat, then you need a more detailed analysis, and the methods for deriving insights might be very different.

- Intuition is relied upon when the event is one-time or the first time. This fundamentally means there is no historical data. For example, when Uber entered the ride-share business, there was not much data available to analyze if people would accept this business model.

- When little justification is needed on the decision made, intuition is preferred over data. This typically happens when there are homogenous stakeholders who pretty much think and act alike or when the decision maker's authority or power is high.

- Finally, intuition is used when the impact or the repercussion of poor decision making is low for the stakeholder(s). For many, eating pizza from Pizza Hut or from Domino's Pizza almost tastes the same. For a non-loyalty card, a customer buying gasoline from Shell or Esso gas station is almost the same. This situation normally happens when the products and services are highly commoditized, with very few differentiating factors.

On the other hand, insights driven from data or evidence are applicable in the following situations.

- Leveraging or mining data that is already captured for compliance and operations. Usually, data origination and data capture do not always start with analytics. Data origination and capture mainly start with operations and/or compliance, and analytics is typically pursued when the data volume reaches a critical size. In the table below, a single purchase order record, which is essential for procurement operations and compliance, does not provide much insight. But when there are many purchase orders (four purchase orders in this case), one could get some insights like when the unit price reduces, then more items are ordered or purchased.

Data

Vendor Id	Name	Item Description	Quantity	Price	Unit Price
123	Excellent Inc	Ball Bearing SKF 6085	80	8000	100

Insights

Vendor Id	Name	Item Description	Quantity	Price	Unit Price
123	Excellent Inc	Ball Bearing SKF 6085	80	8000	100
458	Great Works	Ball Bearing SKF 6085	60	7200	120
261	AB Bearings	Ball Bearing SKF 6085	100	9000	90
984	Chinook Engg	Ball Bearing SKF 6085	200	15000	75

Information - More you order, the unit price reduces

Figure 1.2: Data as a source of insight

- When the hypothesis is complex with many interdependent variables, relying on intuition will not necessarily work. Research has shown the number of information pieces that the human mind can hold, and process is 7 ± 2. In other words, most adults can store and process between 5 and 9 items in their short-term memory [Miller, 1956]. So, in the case of complex situations with many interdependent variables, one needs to rely on data and the computing power of machines for running algorithms in deriving insights.

- Finally, data-driven insights are needed when there are varied opinions and biases on the course of action. Instead of depending on people's opinions and even biases, the best course of action is to use data that is based on evidence or facts. Biases play a big role in analytics, and Chapter 12 discusses the seven types of biases that result in bad analytics.

At the same time, data analytics and intuition need not be mutually exclusive. Data analytics can even be used to validate or test the intuition. Basically, the combination of intuition and data analytics can offer holistic insights to the business by looking at the issue from various angles. Research by Nobel laureate, Daniel Kahneman, and his team found that all strategic decisions are basically evaluated using (1) numerical scores for competing options (2) a yes-no decision on whether to choose a specific path [Kahneman et al., 2019]. Fundamentally, insights from data are rational; they are carefully considered, and negative outcomes are weighed. Irrational decisions are quick and based on intuitive judgment. Hence, the best approach for business is to go for a combination of data analytics and intuition, where data and intuition are augmenting each other so that the insights are reliable and accurate for making good and holistic business decisions.

Now, let us come back to the fundamental question - why do insights matter? Benjamin Disraeli, the British statesman and novelist, said, "One who has the most information will have the greatest success." Louis Pasteur, French biologist and chemist renowned for his discoveries of vaccination, said, "Chance favors the prepared mind." In this context, businesses are evolving entities and constantly seek insights to better prepare and adapt themselves to the marketplace. The need for adaptation can come from two scenarios – internal and external. Firstly, from an internal perspective, businesses need insights to learn more about their current operations and find avenues to increase revenues, decrease costs, and mitigate risks. Secondly, from the external perspective, businesses need insights to harness marketplace opportunities, address competition, and ultimately be relevant in the market.

In both these scenarios, for the businesses to make the right decisions and be prepared, they need the best insights to take the organization to the desired state with optimal utilization of resources; in other words, insights provide business efficiencies. To summarize, businesses need insights to make better decisions for three key aspects:

1. Increasing the revenue streams
2. Reducing expenses
3. Mitigating risk.

About business data

What exactly is data? How do you define data? Data is a set of fields with values in a specific format. Though data is plural and datum is singular, in the business world, data can be both singular and plural. Specifically, the five key characteristics of business data are:

- **Collected with an immediate purpose**. Business data is intentionally collected to serve an immediate business need and is used to record a business category, entity, or event related to:

    o Operations like recording a sales contract, running a payroll, performing equipment maintenance, and so on.
    o Compliance on regulations like GDPR (General Data Protection Regulation) and SOX (Sarbanes–Oxley Act), and industry standards like EDI (Electronic data interchange), UNSPSC (United Nations Standard Products and Services Code), PIDX (Petroleum Industry Data Exchange) and ARTS (Association for Retail Technology Standards)
    o Decision making using the insights related to descriptive, predictive, and prescriptive analytics

    Are there cases where data is collected with no immediate purpose or objective? Open data that is freely provided by the government agencies do not have a defined objective. Also, research data (say EU Open data Portal) is nor captured for a specific context or purpose. Both open data and research data are generic and have multiple uses. But one can take that data and use it for a specific purpose. For example, demographics data from Statistics Canada, which is open data, is not defined for a specific purpose. One can take the data and use it based on a specific need. For example, a travel company can use that data on citizens' income to introduce appropriate vacation packages, a university can use the educational qualifications of the citizens and offer relevant academic programs, a retail chain can look at the community population before opening a new store, and so on.

- **Stored in a medium**. Once the data is captured, it is stored in a medium or storage device. These days the data storage is in IT systems, which could be in the cloud platforms like Amazon's AWS (Amazon Web Services) or Microsoft Azure, or the data can be stored in IT systems in the company's own data center.

- **Repetitive in nature, i.e., reusable**. Once the data is captured in the IT systems, it can be re-used. For example, once the vendor data is captured, that specific data record can be re-used in multiple purchase orders issued to that vendor.

- **Encoded in a specific format**. The data captured in the IT system is in a specific format. Customer name typically is in text format, date of birth is in DD-MM-YYYY format, SIN (Social Insurance Number) is in numeric format with a hash-function validation, and so on.

- **Data is raw that needs to be processed and analyzed for deriving value.** From the analytics perspective, data is not valuable to the business—it is the actionable insights, relationships, patterns, categorization, inferences, and predictions, which are derived from the data that makes data valuable and monetizable. So, data needs to be processed and analyzed with statistical tools for deriving value.

Coming back to the definition of data discussed above, data has three key attributes – fields, values, and format. Let us take the example of the purchase order (PO) data to explain the three key attributes.

1. Firstly, the PO data has a list of fields like vendor identifier, item, quantity, price, unit of measure (UoM), and so on.

2. Secondly, each of these fields has some value – quantitative or qualitative. Quantitative data can be counted, measured, and expressed in numbers; it is objective and conclusive. Qualitative data, on the other hand, is descriptive, conceptual, and expressed in text, audio, video, and

image formats; it is subjective and exploratory. In the below example, the price field is quantitative and has a value of "8000." The item description field is qualitative and has a value of "Ball Bearing SKF 6085."

3. Thirdly, every field in the PO has the value captured in a specific format. For example, the item description field is captured in text format. The quantity field has the value of "80" in an integer format.

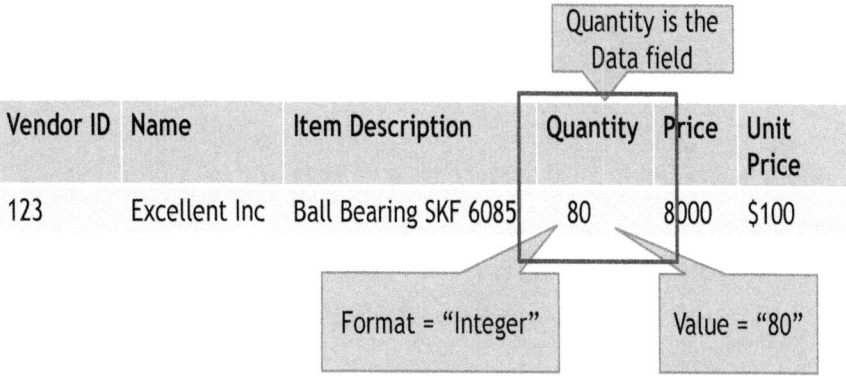

Figure 1.3: Definition of data

Data and competitive advantage

Today, we have evidence to show that data and digital technologies are playing a significant role in shaping the performance of a company. The top five companies in the world in 2019 in terms of market capitalization are from the data and digital technologies sector. These five companies are collectively known as FAAMG, namely, Facebook, Amazon, Apple, Microsoft, and Google. Figure 1.4 shows that the data-centric companies are valued more than the non-data centric companies like Shell and Ford as per the Market-capitalization-Revenue ratio (Y-axis) based on the 2019 data.

The market capitalization of companies is strongly associated with industry sector and digital disruption. In the classic book *Digital Vortex*, authors Tomoko Yokoi, Jialu Shan, Michael Wade, and James Macaulay, define *Digital Vortex* as the inevitable movement of industries toward a "digital center" in which business models, offerings, and value chains are digitized to the maximum extent possible. The *Digital Vortex* is shown in Figure 1.5. The three key findings in their research are:

- Companies in Technology, Retail, Media, and Banking sectors are in the center of the vortex as they are highly vulnerable to digital disruption.
- In the above four industry sectors, digital technologies greatly affect the business models and the value proposition of existing goods and services.
- Digitally disrupted companies are greatly affected by competition from digital and data-savvy players.

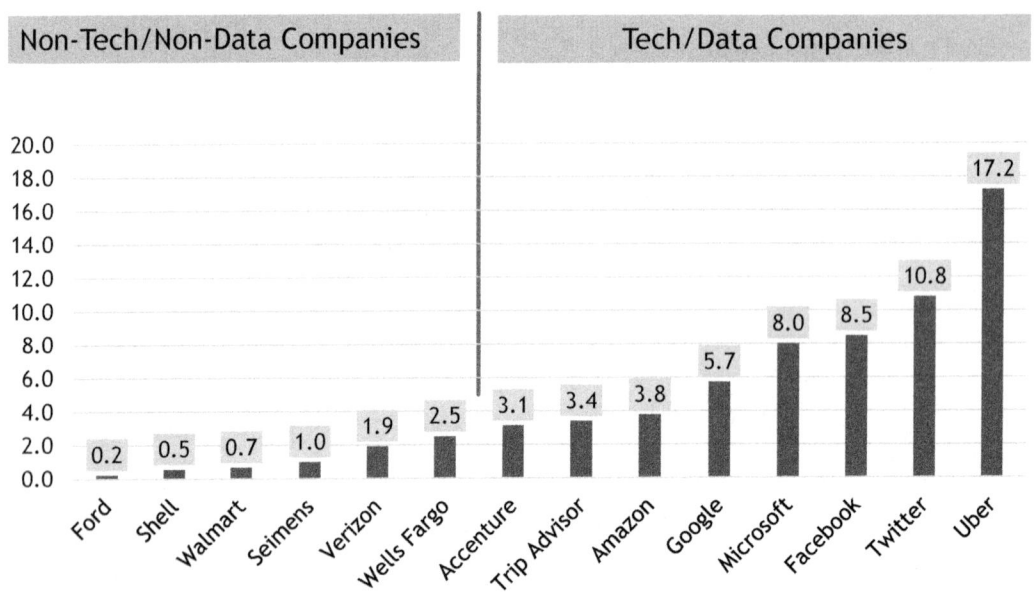

Figure 1.4: Ratio of market capitalization and revenue

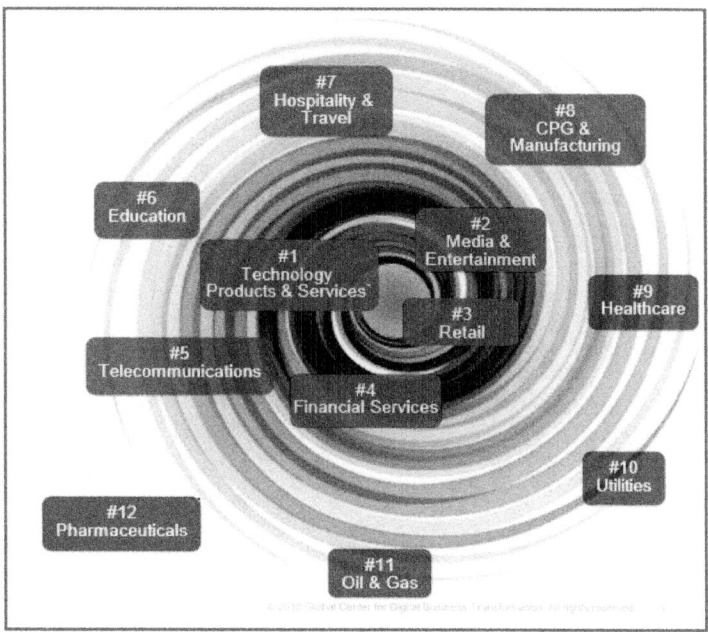

Figure 1.5: Digital vortex

Data and digital technologies are challenging the way organizations operate by creating new consumer expectations, and this shifting of preferences is resulting in companies coming up with innovative products and services. Linking the findings in Figures 1.4 and 1.5, a report from Boston Consulting Group (BCG) has shown that nine out of the top ten innovative companies in the world are from the technology sector [BCG, 2019] – the most digitally disrupted sector in the *Digital Vortex*. This is shown in Figure 1.6.

The above discussion reveals that there is a strong association or relationship between market-capitalization, digital disruption, and business innovation. Technology companies which have a very have large market-capitalization/revenue ratio are not only innovative but are also highly prone to digital disruption.

To thrive, one must be disrupted!

EXHIBIT 1 | 2019 Most Innovative Companies

1	Alphabet/Google	11	Boeing	21	McDonald's	31	AXA	41	Dell
2	Amazon	12	BASF	22	Marriott	32	Unilever	42	Walmart
3	Apple	13	T-Mobile[2]	23	Alibaba	33	Salesforce	43	eBay
4	Microsoft	14	Johnson & Johnson	24	Bayer	34	Pfizer	44	HP Inc.
5	Samsung[1]	15	DowDuPont	25	AT&T	35	Stryker	45	ING
6	Netflix	16	Siemens	26	Allianz	36	NTT Docomo	46	BP
7	IBM	17	Cisco Systems	27	BMW	37	Toyota	47	Daimler[4]
8	Facebook	18	LG Electronics	28	SAP	38	Volkswagen[3]	48	Huawei
9	Tesla	19	Vale	29	Philips	39	3M	49	Rio Tinto
10	Adidas	20	JPMorgan Chase	30	Royal Dutch Shell	40	General Motors	50	Hilton

Source: 2018 BCG Global Innovation Survey.
[1]Includes only Samsung Electronics.
[2]Includes only US T-Mobile, not Deutsche Telekom.
[3]Includes Audi and Porsche.
[4]Includes Mercedes-Benz.

Figure 1.6: Most innovative companies in 2019

The key message from that above discussion is that companies that are digital or data-driven demonstrate improved business performance. A report from MIT says, digitally mature firms are 26% more profitable than their peers [MIT, 2013]. McKinsey Global Institute indicates that data-driven organizations are 23 times more likely to acquire customers, six times as likely to retain customers, and 19 times more profitable [Bokman, 2014]. IDC, a technology advisory firm, predicts that by 2023 half of all GDP (Gross Domestic Product) worldwide will come from digitally enhanced products, services, and experiences [IDC, 2019].

However, just capturing, storing, and processing data will not offer the business a sustainable competitive advantage. Appropriate strategy and positioning of data is also required. The resource-based framework (RBF) is one strategy of deriving competitive advantage. RBF proposes that if a business asset such as data has to offer a sustainable competitive advantage, it must be treated as a resource [Berney,1991]. That means:

- **Data should be valuable**. Data should be highly utilized in business operations, compliance, and decision making – the three key objectives of business data.

- **Data should not be available easily for others or competitors**. One strategy to make data rare is to convert data from a raw format to a processed format. In other words, from unstructured to structured format. Chapter 3 will discuss this topic in more detail.

- **Data should not be substitutable by other types of resources**. For example, intuition is a substitute for data in decision making. If data quality and literacy are poor in the company, intuition will prevail over data in decision making. Chapter 5 looks at data quality, and chapter 7 looks at data literacy in detail.

So, if companies have not worked on building these three core elements in the data strategy, then data will not offer that competitive advantage. For example, the competitive advantage of TripAdvisor is the recommendations data they have on transportation, lodging, travel experiences, and restaurants. TripAdvisor meets the above three criteria; even though on the "Non-substitutable" aspect, there are options to the users from Google, Expedia, and Facebook today. We will revisit the role of data on bringing competitive advantage to the company again in chapter 9 on data monetization.

Data in the balance sheet

If data is such a useful asset for the business, why is data not in the balance sheet of the companies? In financial accounting, an asset is any resource owned by the business that can be converted into cash. An asset has three key characteristics:

1. It holds a probabilistic economic benefit (in the future)
2. It is controlled by the entity
3. The current value of the asset is associated with prior events or transactions.

So, as data meets all the three characteristics and improves business performance, why is it that an intangible asset like data is not in the company's balance sheet? Under the present business and regulatory circumstances, five key reasons make it challenging for data to find a place in the balance sheet.

1. **Costing.** Any asset listed on a company's balance sheet should have an identifiable fair market value (FMV). While many companies talk about data as a monetizable asset, they struggle to put a monetary figure both on the cost of data management in the data lifecycle (from origination to consumption) and the benefits that data brings to the organization. Equipment or a building is assessed by two independent assessors that would pretty much land on the same monetary figure. But calculating the costs and benefits pertaining to data is challenging as the useful life of data in a company spans multiple periods.

2. **Depreciation.** When tangible assets like machinery age, they lose their value, i.e., depreciate. But when data assets age, they can lose or gain value. For example, when master data (which represent business entities such as customers and products) age, it gains its relevance and value as these data objects are usually shared and reused in the enterprise. But when transactional data (which represents business events such as orders, invoices, and deliveries) age, it loses its relevance and its value. In addition, if the data is incorrect and its useful life is just a few days or

weeks, then data cannot be properly depreciated or amortized. This requires specific depreciation methods and regulations which we lack today.

3. **Context.** Assets that are listed on a company's balance sheet are usually utilized in a similar manner at all times. For example, equipment would be used by two different companies in almost the same manner. The same cannot be said of data as data is largely contextual. For example, if a utility company with 1 million historical customer invoices gets acquired by another utility company, the value of these invoice data records for the acquirer is very marginal, who would be bringing their own finance-related policies and procedures.

4. **Capture.** As per IFRS (International Financial Reporting Standards) and GAAP (Generally Accepted Accounting Principles) accounting principles, any asset listed on a company's balance sheet should be an acquired or captured asset. For example, even though an intangible asset such as Apple's logo carries a huge name recognition value, it does not appear on Apple's balance sheet because the logo was developed internally by Apple and was not acquired.

5. **Compliance.** Data can very quickly transform itself from an asset to a huge liability if it has poor security and privacy compliance. While tangible assets like machinery or buildings can also become a liability for a company, the rate of change in the asset to liability conversion in an intangible asset like data is significantly higher and faster compared to a tangible asset. Cambridge Analytica, a company that thrived on data, filed for insolvency and closed operations in May 2018 within two months of the Facebook data breach issue.

Basically, an intangible asset like data brings subjectivity into asset valuation; and businesses loathe unpredictability and vagueness and see it as a risk. Risk mitigation is one of the core objectives of business management. However, data can potentially find a place in the balance sheet if the monetary value can be assigned to the data assets. In fact, the American Telecom company AT&T placed customer lists, an intangible asset, in its balance sheet in 2011 for US$ 2.7 billion USD. In this backdrop, the data monetization field has significantly matured in the last few years. The key is assigning the monetary value to the data asset, which is the first step in data's journey towards finding a place in the balance sheet.

> Strategy focuses on vision
>
> Tactics focus on execution
>
> Tactics consume company's resources
>
> Success is 10 % strategy and 90 % execution

About analytics best practices

As data plays an important role in the performance of a business enterprise, many companies are looking at ways for deriving insights from data using data analytics. But unfortunately, not many are successful. Organizations are now looking for best practices on how analytics initiatives are performed reliably and efficiently. A best practice is a guideline or idea that has been generally accepted as superior to any alternatives because it produces results that are prescriptive, superior, and reusable.

Best practices have served as a general framework in a variety of business situations across numerous industry sectors. For instance, in financial accounting, the generally accepted accounting principles (GAAP) represent best practices for a company to disclose in its financial statements so that investors can analyze and extract useful information. The health care industry relies on best practices guidelines (BPGs) on areas such as Health Technology

Assessment (HTA), Evidence-Based Medicine (EBM), and Clinical Practice Guidelines (CPGs) to offer quality care to patients.

Overall, a best practice tends to be accepted throughout the industry after repeated evidences of success have been demonstrated. They are simply the best way to do things. However, the implementation of the best practices is challenging. According to the American Productivity & Quality Center (APQC), the three main barriers to the adoption of a best practice are [APQC, 2019]:

- lack of awareness and knowledge about current best practices
- lack of motivation required to make changes for their adoption, and
- lack of knowledge and skills required to implement the best practice.

While there is an acceptance of leveraging the best practices at the strategic levels, implementation of it fails at the tactical level. This means a recommended best practice should address the above elements at a tactical level where business resources can be deployed to execute as per the strategy. They say business results are a combination of 10% strategy and 90% execution. While strategy elements such as culture, governance, and senior management support are all important, execution aspects bring the strategy to life.

In this backdrop, there are ten key analytics best practices that can improve the odds of delivering enterprise data analytics initiatives successfully. The implementation of these ten best analytics practices presented in this book is in a playbook fashion – a combination of strategy and tactical elements to deliver the greatest value to the business. Fundamentally, a playbook reflects an approach or strategy defining predetermined responses worked out ahead of time-based on industry best practices for getting things done.

These best practices are compiled from literature study, validation with analytics experts and deployment experience on numerous analytics initiatives – both successful and failed. Realizing all these ten best practices assumes there is strong support from the senior management. These ten tactical best practices are:

1. Tie stakeholders' goals to questions & KPIs
2. Build a high performing team for analytics
3. Understand the data from the analytics view
4. Source data strategically
5. Make data compliance an integral part of analytics
6. Focus on descriptive analytics for data literacy
7. Use continuous refinement and validation as the mainstay of advanced analytics
8. Leverage analytics for data monetization
9. Support analytics with data governance
10. Implement insights with data storytelling and change management

Implement these ten best practices sequentially, as there is a strong dependency on the preceding best practice(s) in the analytics value chain. The analytics value chain is a set of activities designed to deliver insights that answer the business questions. While each step in the analytics value chain requires additional work, it also yields additional value. The mapping of the analytics "Needs-Data-Models-Insights-Efficiencies" value chain to the above ten best analytics practices (BP) appears in the figure below.

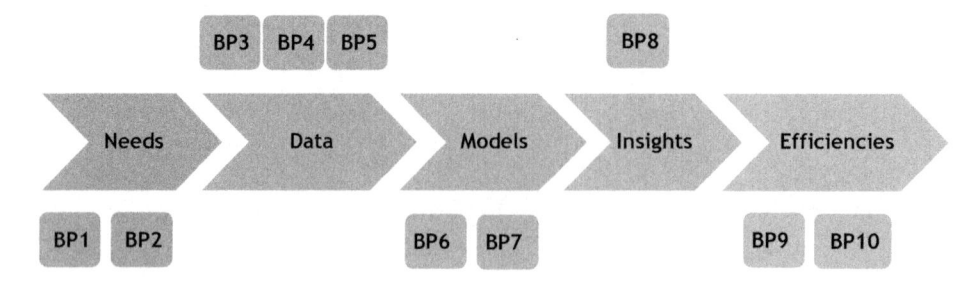

Figure 1.7: Analytics value chain and best practices

The coming chapters will look at implementing these ten best analytics practices in a playbook fashion. Fundamentally, a playbook is a set of predetermined responses worked out ahead of time-based on industry best practices for getting things done. In this backdrop, the structure of each of the ten best practices in the next ten chapters is:

- The necessary background required on understanding the best practice,
- the rationale on why it is a best practice, and
- finally, the capability needed for implementing the specific analytics best practice.

Conclusion

In today's digital and data-centric economy, no organization can afford to ignore the value of data and technology. However, for a business enterprise to be considered as data-driven, it should maximize the value of data and treat data as a strategic business asset. Analytics is a key enabler that transforms data into a business asset by providing insights as inputs for sound decision making. However, not many organizations are successful in transforming their data into insights, and these ten best analytics practices discussed in this book will help to deliver analytics initiatives reliably and efficiently.

References

- APQC, Six Potential Barriers to the Transfer of Best Practices, https://bit.ly/2UvFWca, Nov 2019.
- Ariely, D, "Predictably irrational: The hidden forces that shape our decisions," HarperCollins, 2010.
- BCG, "The Most Innovative Companies 2019," https://on.bcg.com/39tomKp, 2019.

- Bokman, Alec; Fiedler, Lars; Perrey, Jesko; Pickersgill, Andrew, "Five facts: How customer analytics boosts corporate performance," https://mck.co/2Ju0xYo, Jul 2014.
- Brittany, W, "Goldman Sachs – A Technology Company?," https://hbs.me/3dGQWet, Apr 2018.
- Brynjolfsson, Erik and Collis, Avinash, "How should we measure the digital economy," Harvard Business Review, Nov 2019.
- Barney, Jay, "Firm Resources and Sustained Competitive Advantage," Journal of Management, March 1991.
- Haller, Eric and Satell, Greg, "Data-Driven Decisions Start with These 4 Questions," Harvard Business Review, Feb 2020.
- IDC, "IDC FutureScape Outlines the Impact "Digital Supremacy" Will Have on Enterprise Transformation and the IT Industry," https://bit.ly/3azGSSq, Oct 2019.
- Kahneman, Daniel; Lovallo, Dan; and Sibony, Olivier, "A Structured Approach to Strategic Decisions," MIT Sloan Management Review, Mar 2019.
- Mckinsey, "Unlocking success in digital transformations," https://mck.co/2UvGoXV, 2018.
- Miller, George, "The Magical Number Seven, Plus or Minus Two: Some Limits on our Capacity for Processing Information," Psychological Review, 1956.
- Miranda, Gloria Macías-Lizaso "Building an effective analytics organization," https://mck.co/3417wl2, Oct 2018.
- MIT, "Digitally Mature Firms are 26% More Profitable Than Their Peers," https://bit.ly/2xBTPNe, Aug 2013.
- Olavsrud, Thor, "Even Data-Driven Businesses Should Cultivate Intuition," https://bit.ly/2vZ8gu6, Jun 2014.
- Siegler, MG, "Eric Schmidt: Every 2 Days We Create As Much Information As We Did Up To 2003," https://tcrn.ch/2Uz4Ckm, Aug 2010.
- White, Andrew, "Our Top Data and Analytics Predicts for 2019," https://gtnr.it/2yipnrC, January 2019.

CHAPTER 2

Best Practice #1

Tie Stakeholders' Goals to Questions and KPIs

> *"Get closer than ever to your customers. So close that you tell them what they need well before they realize it themselves."*
>
> — *Steve Jobs*

This chapter looks at the first of the ten best analytics practices for a business enterprise. What is a business enterprise and what are its characteristics? A business enterprise is the undertaking of activities associated with the production, sale, or distribution of products or services for its customer(s). A typical business enterprise has three key characteristics.

1. It must address the needs of the market or the customer
2. It must seek to create value for its investors, customers, and other stakeholders
3. It should engage employees to work together in an organized way to produce results for its stakeholders.

In other words, there is no business enterprise without a customer or stakeholder, and every business activity can be attributed directly or indirectly to serve the needs of the stakeholder. Hence like in any other business initiative, in data analytics initiatives too, stakeholders and their insight needs hold the key to successful business results. An analytics initiative is deemed successful when it meets or exceeds the expectations of the stakeholders - individual, group, or organization. While there are many stakeholders who have an interest in the analytics initiative, the key stakeholders are the ones who will be making business decisions consuming the insights derived from the analytics solutions.

With this backdrop, for a business enterprise to conduct itself in a purposeful way, it must first specify the goals for itself, implement them, and then it must track those goals to the actual results. Unfortunately, businesses worldwide are investing heavily in analytics without obtaining the expected ROIC (return on invested capital). Defining clear goals is the first step in analytics initiative as goals define the outcome. The more carefully and clearly one defines the goals, the more likely they are to do the right things and achieve what they wanted to accomplish. Research by Bain consulting found that 30% of the executives said they lack a clear strategy and goal for embedding data and analytics in their companies [Brahm and Sherer, 2017]. Thus, the goals for analytics initiatives should be stated as clearly and critically as possible. But how does one do that?

Though there are many ways to define goals for analytics initiatives, strengthening the goal statement, and aligning the goal statement to the working culture of the company is very important. One way to clarify and strengthen the goal statement is by asking the right questions, and aligning it to the working culture of the organization. One indicator of understanding the working culture of the company is the way the company uses its KPIs (key performance indicators) in its business operations. By mapping business goals to the questions and to the KPIs, organizations can form an accurate and holistic picture of the business environment and the needs of the stakeholders. In a line, goals state the purpose, questions provide the context and depth, and KPIs align the objectives to the working culture.

According to Donald Sull and Charles Sull in MIT Sloan Management Review, to execute strategy, leaders must set ambitious goals, translate them into specific metrics and milestones, make them transparent throughout the organization, and discuss progress frequently. They found that four core principles underpin effective goal systems, and they summarize these elements with the acronym FAST. Goals should be embedded in **frequent** discussions, **ambitious** in scope, measured by **specific** metrics and milestones, and **transparent** for everyone in the organization to see. [Donald Sull and Charles Sull, 2018].

> *Payer of Invoice is not the main customer — the consumer of insights is the main customer in analytics!*

It is not enough to just define a high-level goal statement. What is needed is a clear and tangible goal statement. While businesses worldwide are investing heavily in analytics, half of all analytics models developed are never deployed [Coombs, 2019]. Why? One of the key reasons is not asking the right questions and unable to apply insights on business operations. In the field of analytics, this is known as the last mile of analytics (LMA), which is deriving insights and making decisions for better business performance.

According to Chris Brahm and Lori Sherer of Bain Consulting, "we see clients struggling in the last mile. That is the gap between a great analytic output and the actual changed behavior that creates value in the enterprise" [Brahm and Sherer, 2017]. The analytics deployment process adapted from the work of SAS-Institute, the leader in analytics software, is shown in Figure 2.1 [Grover, 2019]. This deployment process aligns with the analytics value chain "Needs-Data-Models-Insights-Efficiencies" discussed in chapter 1.

Why is this a best practice?

Data, insights, and knowledge resources are often distributed within and across business enterprises. Strong business performance rests upon the ability of the business enterprise to share and use the data and insights efficiently [D'Aubeterre et al., 2006]. Many analytics initiatives spend a considerable amount of time on stakeholder analysis, that is, identifying the key analytics stakeholders and understanding their insight needs. But who is a stakeholder? According to PMI (Project Management Institute), a formal definition of a stakeholder is: "individuals and organizations who are actively involved in the initiative, or whose interests may be positively or negatively affected as a result of execution or successful completion of the initiative" [PMI, 2017].

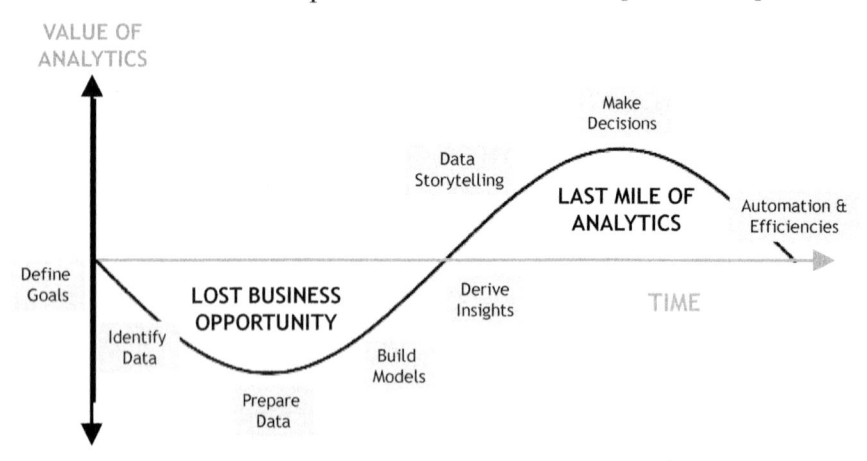

Figure 2.1: Operationalizing analytics

But often in a business enterprise, the insight needs of the stakeholder are complex, varied, and diverse, and these competing requirements when translated into goal statements become generic and vague. The goal statement should consider the stakeholder needs or goals, and once defined, be refined and strengthened by asking appropriate questions, which are validated using the right KPIs. So basically, the stakeholder needs should be based on a goal statement and refined with questions and KPIs.

But what exactly is a goal? A goal is a desired result that a person or an organization envisions, plans, and commits to achieve within a finite amount of time in an environment. The goal defines the context of the problem or the opportunity statement. Clearly, goal setting in an enterprise can address problems and improve business performance. According to Douglas Hubbard, author of *How to Measure Anything: Finding the Value of Intangibles in Business*, "A problem well stated is a problem half solved."

Once the goal is formulated, it can be refined by asking good questions. Questions are the simplest and most effective way of eliciting information. Eric Schmidt, the former CEO of Google, said - "We run Google on questions, not answers." According to Eugène Lonesco, French playwright "It is not the answer that enlightens, but the question." French writer, historian, and philosopher Voltaire said - "Judge a person by their questions rather than by their answers." According to business management guru Peter Drucker, "the important and difficult job is never to find the right answer; it is to find the right question. [Dyer et al., 2011]." According to Edwards Deming, "If you do not know how to ask the right question, you discover nothing" [Lippitt, 2019]. According to Alison Brooks and Leslie John in their Harvard Business Review article, "questioning is a uniquely powerful tool for unlocking value in organizations: It spurs learning and the exchange of ideas, it fuels innovation and performance improvement, it builds rapport and trust among team members. And it can mitigate business risk by uncovering unforeseen pitfalls and hazards" [Brooks and John, 2018]. In short, questions in analytics initiatives help in strengthening the stakeholder goals.

> Design thinking is a human-centric, iterative process to understand the user, challenge assumptions, and redefine problems.
>
> It is made up of five core phases: empathize, define, ideate, prototype, and test.

Once the business goals are strengthened with good questions, the goal can be further validated with pertinent KPIs used by the business. KPIs are usually a reflection of a company's strategic objectives in driving business results. If a business is using KPIs to measure its performance, those KPIs typically drive business behavior, results, and the organization culture.

Hence in the context of analytics initiatives, one must ensure that the insights derived align with the KPIs as these KPIs influence user behavior and the organization's working culture. To summarize, associating the stakeholder's goals to questions and KPIs helps in clearly defining the goals of the analytics initiatives in the enterprise and increases the likelihood of the initiative's success and adoption in the organization.

Realizing the best practice

As discussed in chapter 1, implementing the analytics best practice rests on having the motivation and the pertinent skills associated with the implementation. Realizing this best practice rests on three main strategies or capabilities.

1. Identify stakeholder's business and analytics goal
2. Strengthening the goal statement with pertinent questions
3. Refining the strengthened goal statement with KPIs

"Without context, words and actions have no meaning."
Gregory Bateson, English Anthropologist

1. Identify stakeholder's business and analytics goal

First and foremost, involving the stakeholders early in the analytics program will build business engagement upfront. But, how can one define a good analytics goal statement? As stated before, business stakeholders have different roles and priorities, resulting in the insights need of the stakeholder being complex and varied. For example, marketing wants to increase revenues by maintaining high inventories so that the products are readily available when the customer places an order for products. But finance generally prefers to keep product inventory low so that inventory holding costs are minimized. So, in this case, it is highly unlikely to have a good goal statement that brings the marketing and finance stakeholders together.

Also, for the most part, business enterprises operate within assumptions and constraints. An assumption is a statement that is presumed to be true without concrete evidence to support it. In the business world, assumptions enable companies to simplify the understanding of the problem and allow the business to move forward in the face of uncertainty. Constraints can be fiscal limitations, location limitations, time limitations, resource limitations, market risks, or any other constraints that adversely affect the achievement of the business goal. In addition, the goals defined should align with the company strategy, corporate goals, and the business roadmap. But where does one get these details for defining the goal statement?

> Making assumptions carries a lot of business risks. One way to mitigate the risks associated with assumptions is to ask lot of good questions.
>
> Good assumptions are the result of good communication and collaboration.

There are two main approaches to define the goal statement. The first one is the conventional or the traditional method of directly eliciting the needs or requirements from the stakeholders or insight consumers using techniques such as questionnaires, brainstorming, and prototyping. The conventional approach assumes that the stakeholders or the stakeholder personas have the information and knowledge to formulate a good goal statement. Creating personas helps one understand the stakeholder needs, experiences, behaviors, and goals in a very concrete manner. But often stakeholders or rather the stakeholder personas are not completely aware of the future strategy of the company. So, where can one get this kind of information? The second approach is the indirect or unconventional approach of eliciting information. There are three sources to get that type of information:

1. Company's financial statements
2. Management discussion and analysis (MD&A)
3. Analysts' calls.

There are four main financial statements of a company: (1) balance sheets; (2) income statements; (3) cash flow statements; and (4) statements of shareholders' equity. These financial statements are like the report card of a business.

- Balance sheets show what a company owns and what it owes at a fixed point in time.
- Income statements show how much money a company made and spent over a period.
- Cash flow statements show the exchange of money between a company and the outside world over time.
- Shareholders' equity statement shows changes in the company's shareholder's ownership over time.

The MD&A presents the plans for the company. MD&A provides an explanation, through the eyes of management, a holistic view of the company's financial performance, market conditions, compliance with laws and regulations, its prospects, and approaches to new projects. Here management also highlights product sales, segment performance, margins, and accounting pronouncements, among other things. Below is a 2019 MD&A report of Proctor & Gamble (P&G), a leading CPG (Consumer Packaged Goods) company, where the company has provided details of its various business segments, its contribution to the overall sales, and other performance measures [P&G, 2019].

Net Sales Change Drivers 2019 vs. 2018 [1]

	Volume with Acquisitions & Divestitures	Volume Excluding Acquisitions & Divestitures	Foreign Exchange	Price	Mix	Other [2]	Net Sales Growth
Beauty	3 %	2 %	(4)%	2%	4%	(1)%	4 %
Grooming	(1)%	(1)%	(5)%	2%	—%	(1)%	(5)%
Health Care	5 %	4 %	(3)%	1%	2%	— %	5 %
Fabric & Home Care	4 %	5 %	(3)%	1%	1%	— %	3 %
Baby, Feminine & Family Care	1 %	1 %	(4)%	1%	—%	— %	(2)%
TOTAL COMPANY	3 %	2 %	(4)%	2%	1%	(1)%	1 %

Figure 2.2: P&G MD&A statement

Lastly, the Analysts' call, which the third unconventional source on understanding the company's future strategy, especially for a publicly-traded company, is another great source of information. Here the company's senior executives share the financial performance and the future direction of the company.

Once the preliminary goal statement is formulated, it can be further refined using the well-known SMART criteria in addition to the FAST criteria that were discussed in the introduction section. The SMART emphasizes that every business objective or goal should be: **S**pecific, **M**easurable, **A**ssignable, **R**ealistic, and **T**ime-related. Here is an example of an analytics initiative goal:

"Enable the merchandising team to make timely decisions to reduce the operational spend by 15% and achieve a customer satisfaction of 95% by December 2022."

2. Strengthen the goal statement with pertinent questions

Once a broad goal statement is formulated, a set of questions can be used to strengthen or clarify the goal. "Question everything," Albert Einstein famously said. As analytics is fundamentally using data to answer business questions, questions are the core component in analytics. Usually, customers know what they want, but they don't know to articulate it well. So, asking specific questions will allow you to glean insights behind the goal statement. In business, good questions can make the difference between a successful and a failed endeavor, and asking good questions is considered one of the most important skills in business.

The questions generated should strengthen the goals in a quantifiable way, help to clarify the goals, and capture the variation in the understanding of the goals that exist among the different stakeholders. So, where and when are we asking those questions? Kick-off meetings or design workshops that are typically held during the initial stages of the analytics initiative can be used to ask questions and clarify the goal. Here stakeholders should be encouraged to ask questions about the business challenge or opportunities and how data analytics can be used to solve the problem. This brings us to the next part, which is, how does one ask good questions? In this backdrop, there are two key question generation techniques that can be used to formulate the right questions.

> Do not assume that customers will always have a clear goal statement. As they say, if Henry Ford asked customers what they wanted, they would have said faster horses!

1. 5WH Framework

The goal statement can be strengthened by asking closed-ended and open-ended questions. Closed-ended or dichotomous questions are those which can be answered by a simple "yes" or "no," while open-ended or exploratory or 5WH questions are those which require more than a simple one-word answer. For answers to these open-ended questions, it is better to get more responses from multiple stakeholders for completeness. Also, getting answers from multiple stakeholders might lead to more powerful questions.

The 5WH are questions whose answers are considered basic in information-gathering. According to the 5WH principle whose origins can be traced to journalism, a report can only be considered complete if it answers these questions. An example of the 5WH framework can be:

- **Who** is the customer?
- **What** did the customer buy?
- **When** did the customer buy?
- **Where** did the customer buy?
- **How** did the customer buy?
- **Why** did the customer buy?

As seen above, while the first five questions have a direct answer, the "Why" question is more powerful and requires thorough analysis before answering. The 5WH framework is as shown below.

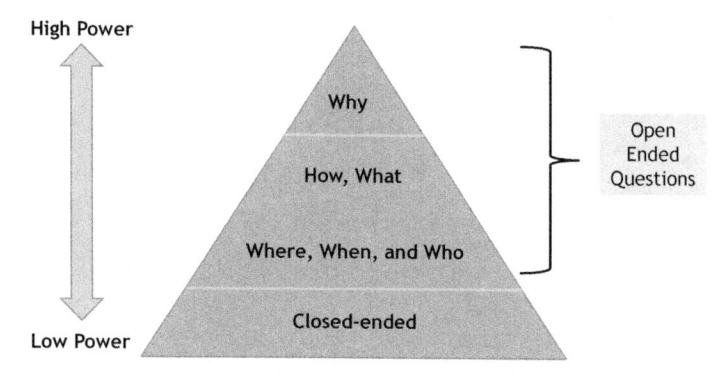

Figure 2.3: 5WH Framework

2. Blooms' Taxonomy

The second question generation technique is Bloom's taxonomy. Bloom's taxonomy, developed by Benjamin Bloom, an American educational psychologist, helps to compose questions on six levels ranging from lower to higher levels of cognitive thinking. The framework consists of six major categories: Knowledge, Comprehension, Application, Analysis, Synthesis, and Evaluation. Below is an example of the application of Bloom's taxonomy in business.

- **Knowledge** - Who are our top five customers by sales orders value?
- **Comprehension** - Compare the performance of the health drink business unit in 2017 and 2018?
- **Application** - What is the impact on quality when the price is reduced by 12%?
- **Analysis** - What are the variables that impact my retail store sales?
- **Synthesis** - What is the impact on sales by consolidating two sales offices?
- **Evaluation**- Can I issue this PO to this new vendor?

> The key functions of business management are leading, planning, organizing, and controlling.
>
> Ensure that the questions asked align to these four key management functions!

However, while eliciting answers from the questions either by using the 5WH framework or Bloom's taxonomy, a few questions might not have clear answers. In that case, hypotheses can be used to explain and answer the phenomena. In business, a hypothesis is an educated guess or intuition one creates prior to running a project based on cause, effect, and rationale. Regardless of whether the questions give clear and definite answers, it is always better to use a hypothesis, as hypotheses help in the derivation of the attributes associated with the goal statement.

The right question(s) reframes the problem or opportunity and forces one to look at it in a different way. But there could be a chance that one might get into the framing trap. While questions are the key to deriving insights in analytics, not framing the question in the right manner can be very dangerous. The framing trap occurs when we misstate a problem, undermining the entire decision-making process. However, one can address the adverse effects of framing bias by employing the following guidelines:

- Pose problems in a neutral or unbiased way
- Always try to reframe the problem in various ways at different time frames with different stakeholders in different contexts
- Align the question list to the decision-making process in the organization

3. Refine the goal statement with KPIs

The third strategy to further refine the goal statement is using the KPIs. KPIs drive business performance and the organization's working culture. In other words, KPIs enable actionable insights. According to research by KPI-Institute and Aberdeen group, companies that track performance using KPIs achieve two times higher net-income growth and three times higher sales growth than those companies who do not [KPI-Institute, 2012]. However, in most companies, KPIs not only drive business performance, they also impact employee behavior and the working culture.

How can KPIs affect working culture? For example, some companies use EBITDA (Earnings before Interest, Taxes, Depreciation, and Amortization) as a profitability KPI. Many experts argue that EBITDA is not a great KPI as the cost of doing business should include the taxes paid to the government, the interest that the company pays to the lenders, the depreciation of assets, and other expenses, and these expenses are not factored in the EBITDA. So, one key reflection of a company using the EBITDA metric, is that the company does not focus much on the depreciation of tangible assets like machinery. Simply put, asset management is not a very critical element or priority to these firms in their operation. So, if asset-intensive companies in the Energy and Telecom sectors take EBITDA as the profitability KPI, the company is potentially not focusing on optimizing its assets, thereby affecting the behaviors and the performance of the employees towards asset management.

> **Ask these 5 simple questions to better use the insights.**
>
> 1. Why do you want to know?
> 2. What is the value of knowing and NOT knowing?
> 3. Is the value of the insights significantly higher than the cost of getting insights?
> 4. Who owns and consumes the insights derived?
> 5. Can you act on those insights?

The second example of the impact of KPIs on working culture is related to the implementation of a performance dashboard for an Oil refinery. The KPIs selected in the dashboard were expected to bring financial visibility into the refinery operations. This led to the identification of savings of US$ 8 million/annum for the Oil Refinery. This means the savings could result in OPEX (Operational Expenses) budget for the Refinery Manager slashed by 40%. But the project was not well supported by the Refinery Manager as his promotion and growth in the company was tied to the size of the OPEX budget he managed and not on the productivity savings.

Ultimately analytics initiatives like any other initiatives fail or succeed because of people as ultimately, people deliver results. Knowing the KPIs and their impact on the working culture will help to understand how people are rewarded and recognized. This will help to further fine-tune or refine the goal statement. If the KPIs cannot be changed, then the goal statement needs to be reworked and adapted appropriately without compromising the overall vision or the strategy of the company. If the KPIs do not align with the business goal, new KPIs need to be introduced.

Conclusion

They say, "start with the end in mind." In business, the journey starts by defining or addressing market needs or stakeholder requirements. Basically, there is no business initiative without a customer, and analytics initiatives are no exception. Analytics initiatives should be driven based on the needs of insight consumers. While many data analytics projects do a great job of identifying the business stakeholders and the consumers of the insights, unfortunately, the goals of the insight consumers are often not very clearly and deeply defined and do not align with the larger objectives of the enterprise. The goals can be refined by asking questions, formulating a hypothesis, and ensuring that the goal statement aligns with the performance KPIs. KPIs hold the key to ensuring that the insights derived from the goal statement are actionable. Also, the inadvertent benefit of involving business stakeholders early leads to higher adoption of analytics. This makes organizational change management much easier, thereby improving the odds of success for the data analytics initiative.

References

- Brahm, Chris and Sherer, Lori, "Closing the Results Gap in Advanced Analytics: Lessons from the Front Lines," https://bit.ly/2xG6kah, Aug 2017.
- Brooks, Alison W and John, Leslie K, "The Surprising Power of Questions," Harvard Business Review, May 2018.

- Coombs, Lindsey, "Mystery solved: The case for operationalizing analytics," https://bit.ly/2V3IMVd, Oct 2019.
- D'Aubeterre, Fergle; Singh, Rahul; Iyer, Lakshmi; and Salam, Al, "Semantic Knowledge Integration for eBusiness Processes: An Ontological Analysis," AMCIS 2006.
- Donald Sull and Charles Sull, "With Goals, FAST Beats SMART," MIT Sloan Management Review, Jun 2018.
- Grover, Suneel, "SAS Customer Intelligence 360: Hybrid marketing and analytics' last mile [Part 1]," https://bit.ly/39vJr6P, Aug 2019.
- KPI Institute, "The value of pre-built Performance Dashboard solutions," https://bit.ly/2WTBANT, Feb 2012.
- Lippitt, Mary, "Six Situational Mindsets to Putting First Things First," https://bit.ly/2US8SKu, Aug 2019.
- P&G, https://bit.ly/2JwQbGQ, 2019.
- PMI (Project Management Institute), "A Guide to the Project Management Body of Knowledge," Project Management Institute, Sep 2017.

CHAPTER 3

Best Practice #2

Build the High Performing Analytics Team

"Talent wins games, but teamwork and intelligence win championships."
Michael Jordan

Once the goal statement for the analytics initiative is defined, refined, and validated, implementing best practice # 1, the goal needs to be realized by the analytics team. The second-best analytics practice is on building high performing analytics teams. Whether the company is a big corporation with thousands of employees or a small company with just twenty employees, high performing teams inevitably offer superior business results. "No matter how brilliant your mind or strategy is, if you are playing a solo game, you will always lose out to a team," is the way Reid Hoffman, LinkedIn co-founder, sums it up. Successful analytics initiatives are no exception and are also dependent on high performing teams to provide good business insights to the insight consumers.

Why is this a best practice?

While most companies understand the importance of analytics, according to a recent McKinsey survey, fewer than 20% have maximized the potential and achieved analytics at scale [Miranda, 2018]. There are many reasons for this dismal statistic, and one important reason is the organizational design or team structure for data analytics. This is important in today's business environment as every company is a data company that strives to have an operating model that focuses on innovation, scale, and value creation. Achieving this requires a set-up with new skills, new roles, and new organizational structures.

Building the right data analytics team starts at the highest level in the company. At a strategic or board level, there is still a lack of awareness on the potential of digital technologies on business performance. McKinsey's research says just 16% of the board members fully understand how the industry dynamics of their companies were changing due to digital technologies [Mckinsey, 2018]. At the operational level, most enterprise data analytics teams today are a shadow of the old MIS (Management information system) or BI (Business Intelligence) team structure and typically reporting into the CFO (Chief Financial Officer) function. These "CFO-centric" teams are organized around the specific IT skills that are often a combination of ETL (Extract-Transform-Loading) developers who build and maintain data-marts and data-warehouses, business analysts who capture the needs of business users for operational and BI reports and report builders who run queries and build reports. In addition, most of the current data analytics teams report to the CFO, who is usually averse to innovation and change as it is a cost controlling and regulatory function. This makes it difficult for the analytics team to deviate from this mind-set.

> In the organization structure, the analytics teams should sit closer to the revenue generation functions like sales, operations, or innovation as the goals of these teams are inherently value creation and revenue generation with focus on customers and the market.

Realizing the best practice

There is no one standard way to build a high performing analytics team. Building a strong data analytics team varies from one organization to another and is usually contextual. Some of the characteristics of effective teams like communication, trust, a clear sense of purpose, and mutual support, are applicable to data analytics teams as well. But there are some characteristics that are specific to analytics teams. Top-performing analytics organizations are enabled by deep functional expertise, strategic partnerships, and a clear center of gravity for organizing analytics talent [Miranda, 2018]. These are the strategic elements. But what are the tactical aspects of building a high performing analytics team? Below are five key tactical elements or capabilities that are required in realizing this best practice of building high performing data analytics teams.

1. Data literacy as the foundation
2. A strong analytics leader
3. Staffing the team across the entire data lifecycle
4. Hypothesis-based methodology
5. Execution mechanism for data analytics

This brings us back to the earlier question on where the data analytics team should be positioned in the organization? Should the data analytics team report to the CFO, or should it report to a different function? Fundamentally, data analytics is a value creation function; it is not a controlling or a regulatory function. In other words, the data analytics team and the leader should come from the "create" or customer-facing business functions like Sales, Marketing, Innovation, Operations, or even better – the data team headed by the Chief Data Officer (CDO).

A 2018 KPMG study found businesses that have a CDO are twice as likely to have a clear digital strategy [KPMG, 2018]. According to IBM, two-thirds of the firms that have a CDO outperform rivals in market share and data-driven innovation [IBM, 2016]. Even during the COVID-19 pandemic crisis, the Center for Disease Control (CDC) was looking at recruiting a CDO, and this highlights the importance of the CDO role [Vincent, 2020]. Mario Faria of Gartner Research Board (GRB) says, "Most CDOs care about solutions and how they can impact revenue" [Torres, 2019].

> How many companies would hire a CFO who cannot read a balance sheet? Hopefully none, because they treat money as an asset and want competent and qualified people to manage it.
>
> Similarly, analytics initiatives should be led by a qualified and competent leader as data is also an asset.

1. Data Literacy as the foundation

Along with having the CDO, the success of the enterprise data analytics team rests heavily on establishing a culture of data literacy in the entire organization. Data literacy is essential to position the analytics team for success. Data literacy in the analytics context can be achieved by creating an environment where the organization strives to use insights from data over intuition to augment their decision-making process.

Senior management support is essential for achieving data literacy in the company. But how does one convince the senior management if they lack an analytics background? The C-suite is not always thinking of data analytics as they assume that analytics is covered and managed by the operational team. Tactically, you build awareness on data literacy to the senior management by highlighting the business opportunities lost and the compliance risk that exists due to a lack of data analytics products and solutions in the organization. Business practice #6, discussed in chapter 7, looks at building data literacy in the company, and chapter 9 looks at building data monetization capabilities in the company.

2. A strong analytics leader

Once the culture of data literacy initiative is in place, a strong leader is required on the ground to run the data analytics initiatives. The analytics team should be led by one who has a solid understanding of data, technology, and the business to translate the vision and the needs of the business stakeholders into measurable results. In most organizations today, this analytics leader is the CDO – Chief Data Officer. Just like the CFO manages money, the CMO (Chief Marketing Officer) manages products, the CDO should manage one of the key business assets – data.

According to Florian Zettelmeyer and Matthias Bolling of Kellogg School of Management, "Getting value from data is not a technical challenge. It is a leadership challenge that demands developing and deploying data strategy throughout the organization" [Zettelmeyer and Bolling, 2015]. According to them, the analytics leader role demands excellence in three strikingly different areas:

1. **Strategic orientation**: The analytics leader must be able to find new opportunities to add value, not simply oversee analytics operations.

2. **Change leadership**: This will involve developing processes to break data silos, drive data-driven projects across those functions, and link analytics initiatives to operations.

3. **Collaboration and influencing**: The analytics leader must cultivate a compelling vision, earn buy-in from key stakeholders to weave analytics into the fabric of the organization.

Mckinsey consulting calls the analytics leader as a catalyst—who embraces a style of leadership addressing the current demands and roadblocks and deploys analytics solutions at scale. The analytics leader should have the skills and experience not only to build the culture of data literacy but also to educate and drive implementation of insights throughout the organization.

3. Staffing the team across the entire data lifecycle

Traditional enterprise data analytics teams focus on technical capabilities like ETL (Extract-Transform-Loading data) and report building, while the best analytics practice is to build a multi-disciplinary analytics team across the entire data life cycle (DLC). DLC is the sequence of stages a data element goes through from its initial generation to its eventual archival and/or purging at the end of its useful life. From an analytics perspective, there are four sequential stages in DLC: Data Capture, Data Integration, Data Science, and Data Visualization.

- **Data capture** is on the origination and capture of data in the System of Record (SoR) of the enterprise. Data is typically captured in the transactional systems like ERP, CRM, and PLM. The SoR is an IT system that can serve as an authoritative source of truth for business processes such as Finance, HR, Sales, and Procurement.

> Data Analytics is not a technical problem; it is fundamentally a leadership problem.
>
> The problem is not envisioning, not aligning the team to the vision, and not executing the vision.

- **Data engineering** fundamentally is acquiring business data for analytics. Data engineering is more than data cleansing and includes data formatting, removing duplicates, renaming, correcting, improving accuracy, populating empty data fields, data integration (ETL/EAI), aggregation, blending and other data management activities. The goal of data engineering is to make the quality data available for the data scientists in a canonical database like a data warehouse or data lake to perform analytics and derive insights. Data engineering takes a lot of time and effort, and best practice # 4 looks at some of the reasons.

- **Data science** is applying statistical techniques on the integrated or canonical database to perform the three main types of analytics: descriptive, predictive, and prescriptive analytics. Chapter 12 explains the key statistical techniques in data analytics.

- **Data visualization** is deriving and communicating measurable economic benefits on the insights derived from data for the business enterprise. Chapters 7 and 11 will revisit this topic.

The four stages of the DLC and the key IT products in each of these DLC stages are shown below.

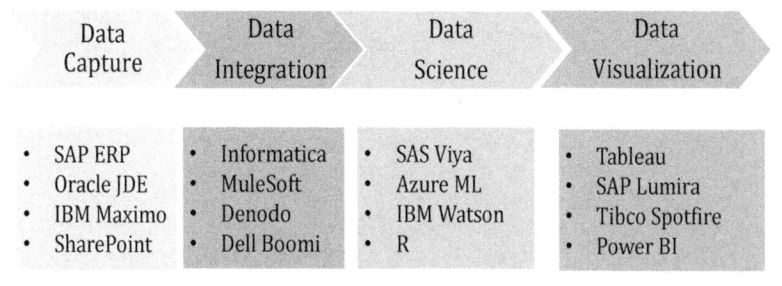

Data Capture	Data Integration	Data Science	Data Visualization
• SAP ERP • Oracle JDE • IBM Maximo • SharePoint	• Informatica • MuleSoft • Denodo • Dell Boomi	• SAS Viya • Azure ML • IBM Watson • R	• Tableau • SAP Lumira • Tibco Spotfire • Power BI

Figure 3.1: Data Lifecycle (DLC)

Value stewardship over showmanship.

With this backdrop, the analytics team should be led by the Product Manager given that the delivery of data-analytics solutions often demands strategic planning, capital investment, and management of complex development cycles, including ongoing maintenance. The emphasis is on product management over project management as analytics product managers focus on scale and reusability, while project managers usually focus on the instantiation of the analytics products in a time-bound manner. An analytics product manager holds the key if the organization intends to be a long-term player in leveraging data analytics for business performance.

This requires the analytics team should constitute team members who bring expertise on data capture, data engineering, data science, and data visualization and should be supported by the data governance team. While the data capture and the data engineering teams are IT teams, the data science and data visualization teams should be from the data team. Regardless, the team members from both these data and IT functions should integrate seamlessly and work collaboratively with business stakeholders.

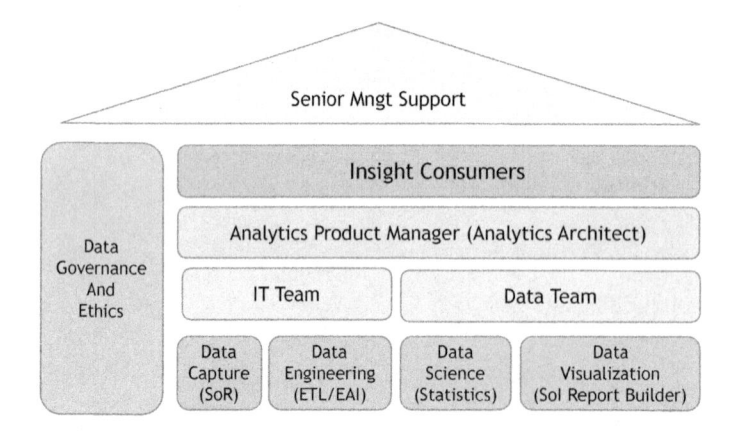

Figure 3.2: Analytics team structure

4. Hypothesis-based methodology

The next phase is to devise a methodology specifically for delivering analytics solutions. Analytics solutions cannot be often delivered in a big-bang approach.

It must be delivered iteratively and incrementally as the business is an evolving entity, continuously adapting itself to be relevant in the market. In this regard, a hypothesis-based methodology will offer the data analytics team early and quick insights and sets the direction for iterative and incremental analytics processes. Fundamentally, the hypothesis-driven approach recognizes that there are multiple possible alternatives for any given problem, and it examines each using data to test and, ultimately, prove or disprove the assertions.

While there are many techniques for developing hypothesis-based thinking, one key technique is the McKinsey's thought process called MECE - an acronym for Mutually Exclusive, Collectively Exhaustive, which separates the problem into distinct, non-overlapping issues while making sure that no issues relevant to the problem have been overlooked. MECE works by grouping elements that are mutually exclusive (ME) and collectively exhaustive (CE), which can then be used to logically categorize issues that can be analyzed systematically and minutely [Chevallier, 2016]. In simple words, MECE ensures that all elements listed cover the entire range of ideas while being unique from each other.

5. Execution mechanism on data analytics

Finally, how will the analytics team deliver? How will this delivery be different from the conventional IT-centric team? The execution mechanism of the analytics team will be different from the conventional IT-centric team in three main ways:

1. They focus on data and the way the data is managed in its lifecycle
2. They translate stakeholder goals into hypotheses and continuously define and redefine the hypothesis that can be verified using data.
3. They deliver insights in an iterative and incremental manner.

In this backdrop, there are three key aspects in delivering or executing data analytics solutions in a business enterprise. Firstly, the analytics team should work closely with business stakeholders who believe in leveraging data for business performance. In some organizations, there might be some managers who are not convinced that data will improve business performance. Instead of educating and convincing these types of managers, it would be more effective to collaborate with leaders who believe in leveraging data for business results to start with.

Secondly, the analytics team should start on a small scale and focus on building trust and credibility with the business. What exactly does *small* mean for a data analytics team? Small could be a small number of use cases, engaging a small number of business stakeholders, working on small data sets with sample data, smaller time frames, small budgets, smaller projects like proofs-of-concept (PoC), and so on. Thirdly, the analytics team should focus on "good enough" analytics solutions. Analytics initiatives will rarely be fulfilling all the needs of all the stakeholders, given that the needs of the stakeholders and varied and diverse. Analytics solutions take refinement in an iterative and incremental manner, and the analytics teams should work on showing some small and significant wins quickly so that they can be positioned for bigger success in the enterprise.

When working on analytics initiatives, think big, start small, and act fast.

Conclusion

Building high performing enterprise data analytics teams is more than staffing people with ETL and report building skills. Today, as data and analytics extend their footprint across the organization, it is very important for all stakeholders to have a shared understanding of what will drive success. The business expectations today from the analytics team are on value creation along with compliance and performance reporting. Since data analytics in business enterprises today is the new language of business communication, the data analytics teams should work on ensuring that the data and insights are in the hands of competent leaders and front-line knowledge workers who will use data and insights to drive better business results.

References

- Chevallier, Arnaud, "Strategic Thinking in Complex Problem Solving," Oxford University Press, 2016.
- Gloria Macías-Lizaso Miranda, "Building an effective analytics organization," https://mck.co/39AKCBY, October 2018.
- IBM, "The Chief Data Officer playbook," https://ibm.co/3aokPx7, 2016
- KPMG, "CIO Survey 2018," https://bit.ly/3etJ68q, 2018.
- Mckinsey, "Unlocking success in digital transformations," https://mck.co/2WZtenQ, 2018.
- Southekal, Prashanth and Raju, Santosh, "Building the High Performing Team for Enterprise Data Analytics," https://bit.ly/2UKS1t6, Dec 2019.
- Torres, Roberto, "Chief data officers of the future sharpen focus on revenue, products," https://bit.ly/2KswcKh, 2019.
- Vincent, Brandi, "During Pandemic, CDC Aims to Hire Chief Data Officer," https://bit.ly/34TF05e, Apr 2020.
- Zettelmeyer, Florian and Bolling, Matthias, "Big Data Doesn't Make Decisions, Leaders Do," Kellogg Initiatives White Paper, 2015.

CHAPTER 4

Best Practice #3

Understand the Data from the Analytics View

> *"Not everything that counts can be counted, and not everything that can be counted counts."*
>
> **Attributed to Albert Einstein**

Data is the fundamental building block of analytics; there is practically no analytics without data. In business enterprises, both big and small data are used in leading, planning, controlling, and operating a business organization that provides goods and/or services to their customers. Specifically, enterprise or business data has three key characteristics.

- **Enterprise data has multiple stakeholders or consumers.** Enterprise data is typically shared and used in business operations across various LoBs (lines of business). As the goals of the LoB vary, the same enterprise data is viewed and consumed differently by different types of stakeholders. For example, the vendor payment terms, which are the established conditions between the vendor and the client organization to settle the payment of invoices, can be Net30, Net60, and so on. For example, Net30 specifies that the net amount to be paid in full by the buyer within 30 days of the date when the goods are received or when the service is completed. These payment terms are usually viewed by the finance department from a cost perspective, while the procurement views the same vendor payment term from a service perspective.

- **Enterprise data is purpose and context-driven.** Fundamentally, the three main purposes of the data are to help businesses in operations, compliance, and decision making. In other words, the purpose of enterprise data is to connect business processes on operations, compliance, and decision making. For example, the vendor payment-term data say Net30 is captured based on the business process established between the vendors and the client. Once the payment-term data is populated and used in the purchase order, the client is committed to honoring those terms in the payment process.

- **Enterprise data has compliance implications.** Enterprise data is subject to compliance requirements – regulatory, industry standards, and internal business rules. Enterprise data has legal implications due to regulations such as SOX (Sarbanes-Oxley), PCI-DSS (Payment Card Industry Data Security Standard), HIPAA (Health Insurance Portability and Accountability Act) and GAPP/IFRS and hence the data has to be securely protected against unauthenticated and unauthorized access. Apart from security, enterprise data is subject to privacy laws such as PIPEDA, GDPR, CCPA, and so on, industry standards like UNSPSC, UPC, PIDX, NACS, etc., and the internal policies of the company. (Refer to appendix 2 for the abbreviations.)

Today businesses are creating huge volumes of data at an astonishing pace. While this offers numerous opportunities for the business, it also presents significant challenges in deriving good insights. One way for businesses to better manage data is to organize or classify the data into appropriate categories, given that classification is an important management function. In this backdrop, from the business perspective, enterprise or business data can be broadly classified into four stakeholder views as shown below.

1. Storage
2. Integration
3. Compliance
4. Analytics

The data classification based on these four views is as shown in the figure below. The storage, integration, and compliance views are usually based on the native or unprocessed state of data. This native data type should be transformed or processed into the fourth view, the analytics view, so that appropriate insights can be derived for decision making.

Storage
- Structured Data
- Unstructured Data

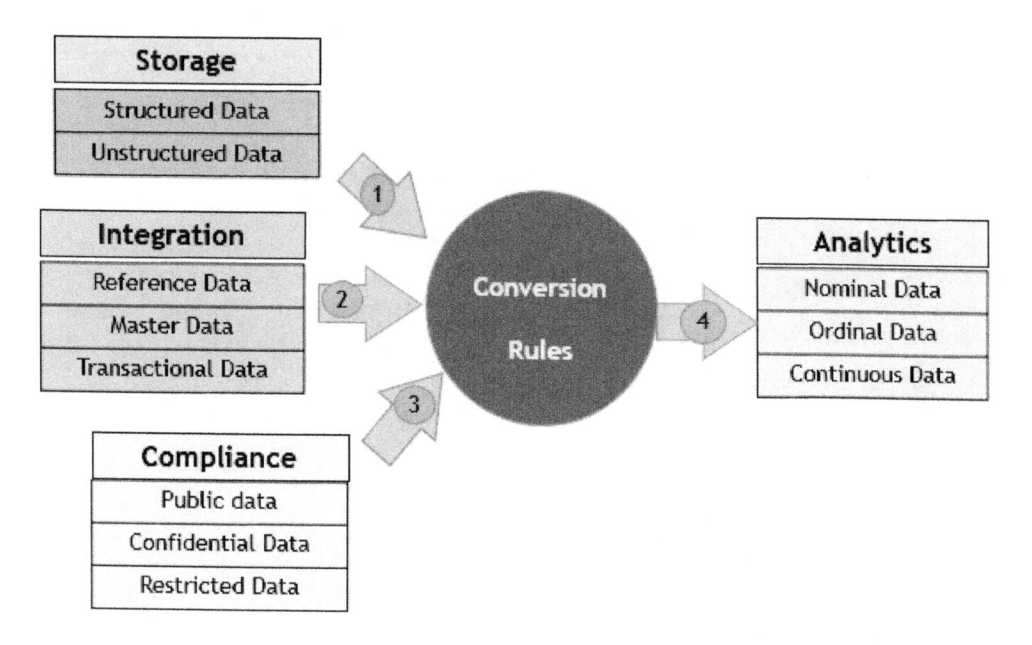

Integration
- Reference Data
- Master Data
- Transactional Data

Compliance
- Public data
- Confidential Data
- Restricted Data

Conversion Rules

Analytics
- Nominal Data
- Ordinal Data
- Continuous Data

Figure 4.1: Types of business data

Classification based on storage

Enterprise data is physically stored in IT systems. There are two main kinds of data storage: primary and secondary. Primary data storage refers to the memory storage that is directly accessible to the processor, such as registers, cache, and RAM (Random Access Memory). Data in the primary data storage is volatile. Secondary storage involves storing data for long-term use. Common examples of secondary storage devices are magnetic disks, optical disks, hard disks, flash drives, and magnetic tapes. However, from the business perspective, storing enterprise data refers to the data stored in the secondary storage devices. The data storage can happen in two main forms - structured and unstructured.

- Structured Data. Data that resides in a fixed format or structure within a database record or file is structured data. Examples are data stored in the database and spreadsheets.

- Unstructured Data. Unstructured data is the data in its native state. That is, data that doesn't have a predefined data structure or format when created. Examples are data in documents, videos, voice, images, etc.

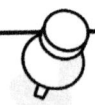

> Whether data is structured or unstructured, data needs to be structured at some point in time in its lifecycle if insights are to be derived. Basically, if the structure of the data is known or fixed during the point of data origination, it is better to capture the data in a structured format.

Incidentally, the majority of the data that is stored in enterprises is unstructured data. Experts estimate that 80% to 90% of the data in any organization is unstructured, and the amount of unstructured data in enterprises is growing significantly — often many times faster than structured databases [Davis, 2019].

Classification based on integration

The second classification view is based on data integration. Businesses serve the needs of the customers by executing business processes. These pertinent business processes, when executed, result in the capture of data as entities, events, and categories. These types of enterprise data reside in different IT systems in different LoB and create a need for an integrated or unified view of the business processes in the enterprise. From the integration point of view, enterprise data can be of three types – reference data, master data, and transactional data.

- Reference data represents business categories such as manufacturing units, currency, stores, and so on. From the software application perspective, reference data is also known as configuration data.

- Master data is a representation of critical business entities such as products, suppliers, assets, and customers. Master data is considered the backbone of the enterprise and is often called the "golden record" or the "single version of the truth." In its truest sense, master data is the single and authoritative source of business data.

Master Data is the foundation for quality data. MDM (Master Data Management) is the process that manages master data in the entire DLC.

Master data generally falls into three types:

1. People such as customers, employees, suppliers, and agencies
2. Things to capture products, parts, devices, equipment, and assets
3. Concepts, including contracts, warranties, General Ledger (GL) accounts, profit centers, and licenses

Transactional data record business events or actions such as purchase orders, invoices, and sales orders. While master data is about business entities (typically nouns), transactional data is about business events (usually verbs).

These three types of data based on integration, reference data, master data, and transactional data, have different levels of reusability. Reference data has high reusability in the company, while transactional data, which is highly contextual to the location, purpose, and time, has low reusability. All three types of data are tied to metadata, which holds technical attributes of the data like type and length. The relationship between the three types of data from the integration point of view is as shown.

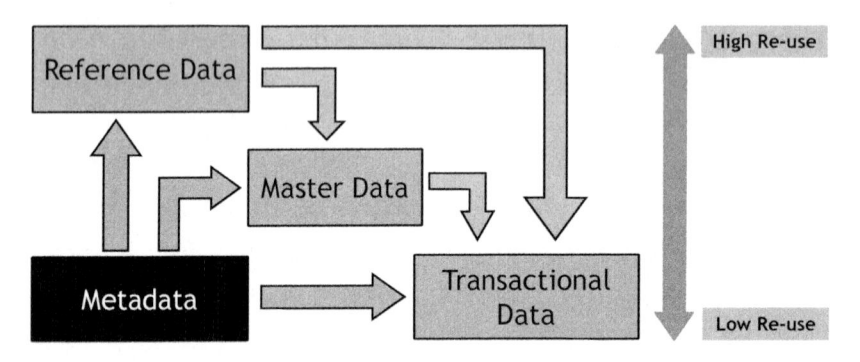

Figure 4.2: Business data based on integration

Classification based on compliance

The third classification view is on data compliance. Inappropriate handling of the business data will have adverse consequences for the business. Hence enterprise data is assigned a level of sensitivity based on the adverse impacts to the business if the data is compromised. Also, the classification of data based on compliance helps determine what baseline security controls are appropriate for safeguarding that data. From the compliance point of view, enterprise data are of three main types: restricted, confidential, and public.

1. Restricted data includes statutory, regulated, and personal data. These data types have the highest level of sensitivity and cover data elements such as SINs, credit card numbers, bank accounts, and health information. Today, data privacy especially is very important in the functioning of the business. Many countries have privacy-related laws and regulations, and examples include the Canadian Personal Information Protection and Electronic Documents Act (PIPEDA), General Data Protection Regulation (GDPR), and the California Consumer Privacy Act (CCPA). These privacy laws recognize the rights of users and address the dangers of the commercial use of personally identifiable data.

2. Confidential data will have medium sensitivity and covers data used for internal business operations such as personnel information, product designs, customer and supplier contracts, sales and purchase orders, and salary slips. Access to confidential data is only to those who have a legitimate business purpose.

3. Public data will have a low level of sensitivity, which makes them easily accessible to anyone. Examples include the company's annual reports, location address, and web and social media pages. This type of data has no restriction on access or usage from copyright, patents, or other mechanisms of control. For example, Open data in Canada provides online access to everyone to the data collected by the Canadian governments.

Classification based on analytics

As said earlier, the above three views of data, storage, integration, and compliance, are usually based on the native state of data. This native data type should be transformed into the fourth view, the analytics view, so insights can be derived for decision making using statistical tools. From the analytics point of view, there are four types of data – Nominal, Ordinal, Interval, and Ratio types.

1. Nominal data are used for labeling or categorizing data. It does not involve a numerical value, and hence no calculations can be done. Examples of nominal data are gender, product description, customer address, and the like.

2. Ordinal data is the order of the values, but the differences between each one is not really known. Common examples here are companies based on market capitalization, vendor payment terms, customer satisfaction scores, goods delivery priority, date/time, and so on.

3. Interval data is about finite numerical values with no zero values. In interval data, if there are zero values, the entity will not exist. For example, the number of employees in a company is interval data. If the number of employees in a company is zero, that means the entity (the company) practically doesn't exist.

4. A ratio scale has all the properties of an interval scale with a meaningful zero. For example, the zero in the company's profit means the company did not make any money, but the company still exists.

Interval and ratio level data types represent numeric or quantitative values. They are amenable to statistical techniques, and these two data types can be grouped together as continuous data – which again could be classified as discrete data or time-series data.

- Discrete data is capturing events that are infrequent or irregular. This is typically created by people based on discrete business events like purchase orders, work orders, invoices, field tickets, PoS (Point of Sale) transactions, and so on.

- Time-series collect data in a regular and more granular manner. A time series is a sequence taken at successive and equally spaced points in time. This data is usually created automatically and have no clear association with business events. In addition, time-series data accumulates very quickly. Examples of time series data are capturing GPS coordinates of a truck every five seconds, capturing machine vibrations every second using the IoT (Internet of Things) infrastructure, and so on.

> Logarithmic scale and linear scale are the two most common types to show changes in numeric or continuous data.
>
> Logarithmic scale show percentage of value change while linear scale show the absolute value change.

So, from the analytics view, data can be of three main types – nominal, ordinal, and continuous. The business data taxonomy based on four classification views is shown below.

Business Data Views

Processing View	Integration View	Security View	Analytics View
Structured Data	Reference Data	Public Data	Nominal Data
Unstructured Data	Master Data	Confidential Data	Ordinal Data
	Transactional Data	Restricted Data	Continuous Data
			Discrete Data / Timeseries Data

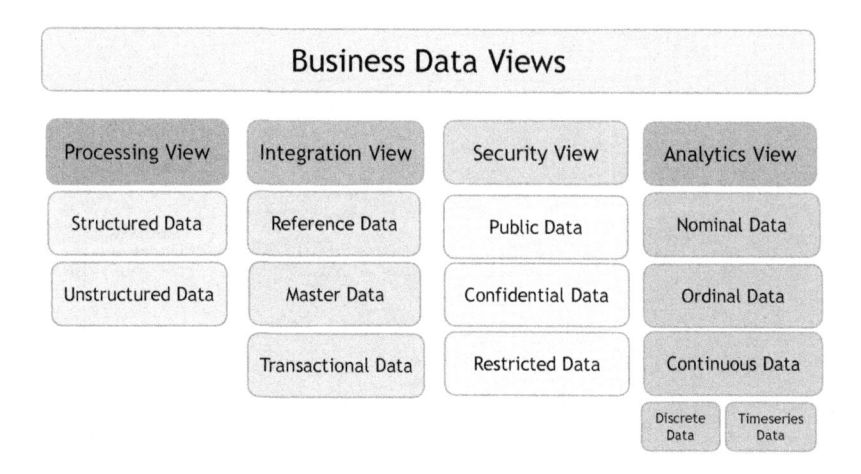

Figure 4.3: Business data taxonomy

Regardless of the four types of views, all the data types are tied to the metadata. Metadata is used to describe another data element's characteristics or attributes; metadata is simply "data about data," and not the data that is used by the business. Metadata is further is classified into three types:

1. Technical metadata is used to describe data structures or technical aspects. Examples are field length, type, size, and so on.

2. Business metadata is used to describe the non-technical aspects of the data and their usage. Examples are report name, document name, class, document type, and others.

3. Log metadata, which describes details on how, when, and by whom the data object was created, updated, or deleted. Examples are timestamp, created date, created by, changed date, and so on.

Metadata alone has no real business utility and is always married to one or more of the above four views of data. But from a data management perspective, metadata is very useful, especially during data integration and is the foundation of digital asset management (DAM), a mechanism to store, share, and organize digital assets in a central location. Figure 4.4 shows an example from the SAP ERP system where the log metadata is on the sales orders.

ID	Date	Item	SLNo	Sales Promotion	U
▫	17.11.2014			Total incompletion status of all items: Delivery changed	V
▫	19.11.2014			Released credit value of the document changed	L
▫	19.11.2014			Release date of the document determined by credit management changed	L
▫	19.11.2014			Credit management: Risk category changed	L
▫	19.11.2014			Overall status of credit checks changed	L
△	17.11.2014	10		Price has been created	V
▫	17.11.2014	10		Rounding Difference changed	V
▫	17.11.2014	10		Net price changed	V
▫	17.11.2014	10		Item credit price changed	V
▫	17.11.2014	10		Item credit price changed	V
▫	17.11.2014	10		Condition pricing unit changed	V
▫	17.11.2014	10		Net price changed	V

Changes in Request 0002596377

Figure 4.4: Log metadata in SAP ERP

Figure 4.5 contains another example, where a Retail tech start-up in Silicon Valley - Glisten has a solution to automatically translate a product image into detailed metadata with advanced computer vision techniques.

Data enrichment for product data.

Automatically translate a product image into detailed metadata with advanced computer vision techniques.

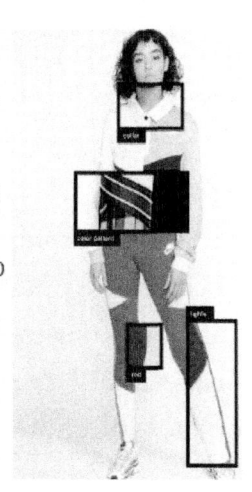

Figure 4.5: Product image metadata

Why is this a best practice?

As mentioned in the earlier sections of this chapter, the three ways of viewing or classifying data based on storage, integration, and compliance are usually done when the data is captured in the native or inherent state. But if the data needs to be consumed for analytics in decision-making, it should be transformed or mapped into the analytics view so insights can be derived using statistical analysis.

But why should one transform the data into an analytics view, that is, nominal, ordinal, and continuous data types? For example, if the data in the native format is qualitative in nature, that is, in the nominal data or categorical data format, that data will not be subject to statistical analysis. Continuous data types, such as interval and ratio data types, offer capabilities for statistical analysis using statistical tools such as averages, standard deviations, t-tests, regression, and ANOVA (Analysis of variance). This helps in deriving precise, objective, and accurate insights.

So the nominal data type is simply used to classify data, ordinal data types are used to order data, and continuous data types, such as interval data and ratio data types, provide capabilities for statistical analysis. Fundamentally, continuous data types are much more definite and precise. This objectivity from the continuous data type improves the legitimacy of the insights derived. Hence, statistical analysis is popular in almost all areas of the business, including strategy, marketing, finance, production, supply chain, costing, IT, legal, and human resources (HR). The table below is the mapping of the three analytics data types, nominal, ordinal, or continuous data types, to the key statistical operations.

		Data Type		
		Nominal	Ordinal	Continuous
Statistical Operations	Mode, Count	Yes	Yes	Yes
	Median, Range		Yes	Yes
	Mean, Standard Deviation, and Standard Error			Yes

NOTE: Standard Deviation and Standard Error are two key measures of data variation. Standard Deviation is a measure of data accuracy, while Standard Error is a measure of precision in data.

Realizing the best practice

How does one realize this best practice? Transforming the native data to the consumption view, that is, the analytics view, has three main steps.

1. Profiling the enterprise data
2. Transforming the native data to the analytics view
3. Balancing the cost and business value in the different analytics data types

Profiling the enterprise data

According to Ralph Kimball, a world-renowned BI expert, data profiling is a systematic analysis of the data [Kimball 2008]. In the business context, data profiling is the process of reviewing the data source, and understanding the data structure, type, content, and interrelationships between attributes, volume, the ingestion mechanism. Data profiling is important as it provides useful insights for understanding the data well. In addition, data profiling insights can be used to improve the quality of data so that the insights derived from analytics are reliable.

Data profiling is not a one-time activity; it is an ongoing exercise as part of continuous improvement.

Broadly there are three key steps in profiling business data.

- Column profiling counts the number of times every value appears within each column or attribute of the database table.

- Cross-column profiling looks across columns in the table to perform primary key (PK) and foreign key (FK) dependency analysis and to determine the dependent relationships within a data set. The PK uniquely identifies a record in the table, while the FK is a field in the table that is the PK in another table. A simple PK-FK relationship in the context of reference, master and transactional data is in Figure 4.6.

- Cross-table profiling looks across tables to identify potential foreign keys. It also attempts to determine the similarities and differences between the database tables to determine which data might be redundant and which could be mapped together.

CUSTOMER TABLE		ITEM TABLE		STORE TABLE		CURRENCY TABLE	
Customer ID (PK)	Name	Item ID (PK)	Name	Store ID (PK)	Name	Currency (PK)	Country
1234	ABC	823	Bearing	AB123	Calgary	CAD	CA
1237	XYZ	857	Valve	ON456	Madrid	EUR	ES

Reference and Master Data Tables

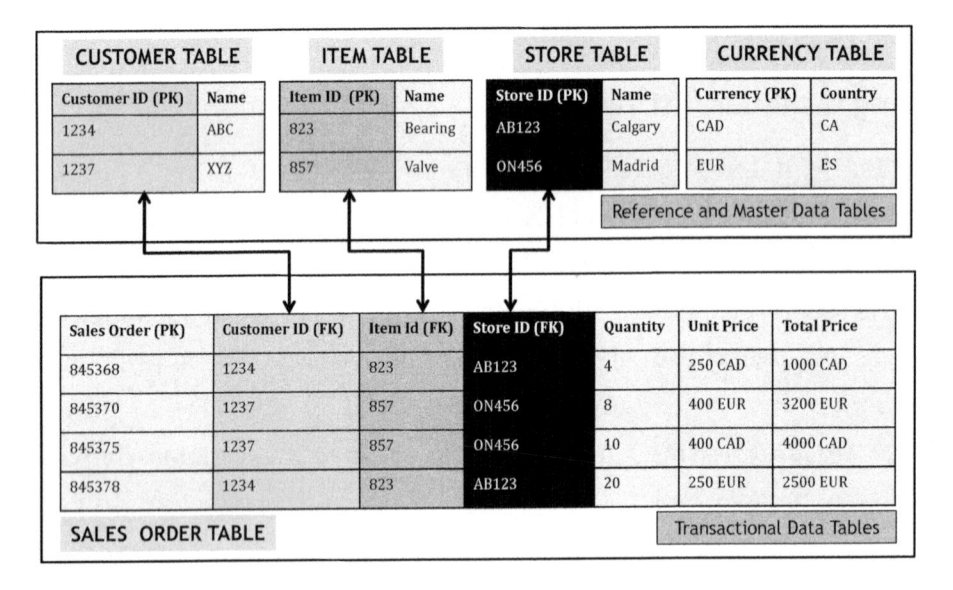

Sales Order (PK)	Customer ID (FK)	Item Id (FK)	Store ID (FK)	Quantity	Unit Price	Total Price
845368	1234	823	AB123	4	250 CAD	1000 CAD
845370	1237	857	ON456	8	400 EUR	3200 EUR
845375	1237	857	ON456	10	400 CAD	4000 CAD
845378	1234	823	AB123	20	250 EUR	2500 EUR

SALES ORDER TABLE — Transactional Data Tables

Figure 4.6: Data integrity in tables

The outcome of data profiling is the data catalog. A data catalog is an inventory of data assets in the organization. The catalog provides the context to understand relevant datasets for extracting business value efficiently.

Transforming the data into the analytics view

As data profiling gives a good understanding of the data, the second capability is on the mechanics of transforming the data into the analytics view. Functionally, data, when it is originated and captured, is mainly for compliance and operational activities. This is the native state of the data; data is rarely originated and captured for analytics. Analytics in business is usually a by-product of compliance and operational activities.

For example, the KYC (Know Your Customer) feature in the Indian Banking industry was started for financial compliance, that is, to address financial fraud and money laundering. But today, the same customer data from KYC is used extensively for customer analytics by the Indian banks. Another example is on vendor purchase orders, which is an operational contract between the company and the supplier. But solid spend analytics depends on a good number of "operational" purchase data records. If the data needs to be used effectively for analytics, the data should be transformed from compliance or operational views into the analytics view.

Analytics data types, that is, nominal, ordinal, or continuous data types, which are subject to statistical analysis, derive precise and accurate insights. For example, a text-based or qualitative data in a purchase order might be good for compliance and operations, but the text-based purchase order data is not effective for analytics. The qualitative or text-centric description will not provide insights as effectively compared to numeric or quantitative data. But if the purchase order is structured with the item code (nominal data), payment terms (ordinal data), and price (continuous data), then much more insights can be derived. Text-based unstructured data is quite common in business enterprises as inspection reports, contracts, emails, social media comments, and customer complaints are all text-based unstructured data. Figure 4.7 is an example where an invoice is in an unstructured or document format, that is, a native view, is transformed into a structured data or analytics view.

Native View - Unstructured Data

Analytics View (Structured Data)

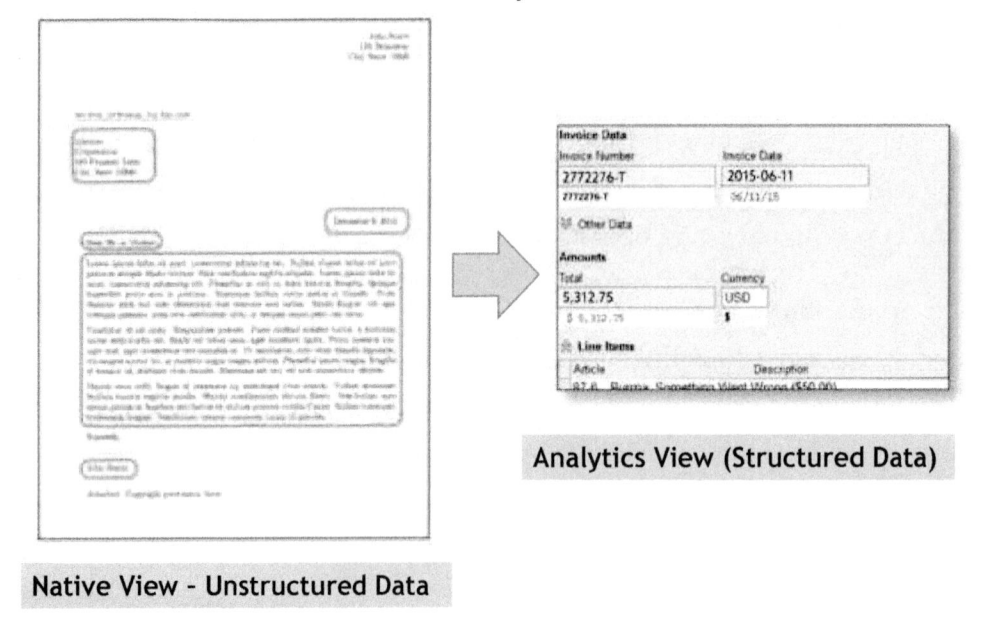

Figure 4.7: Native view to analytics view

So, what are the techniques to transform unstructured or text data into structured data? This process of deriving insights from text-based content is known as text analytics or text mining. There are six key techniques in text analytics, and Figure 4.8 is the flowchart for applying these six concepts.

1. Information Retrieval and Extraction - Analyze unstructured text and find out the keywords, and phrases
2. Categorization/Classification - Classify text under one or more categories.
3. Clustering - Group text content with similar contents
4. Natural Language Processing (NLP) - Enabling computers to analyze and understand human language.
5. Summarization - Reduce the length of the document and summarize the details

6. Visualization - Simplify the process of finding/displaying relevant information.

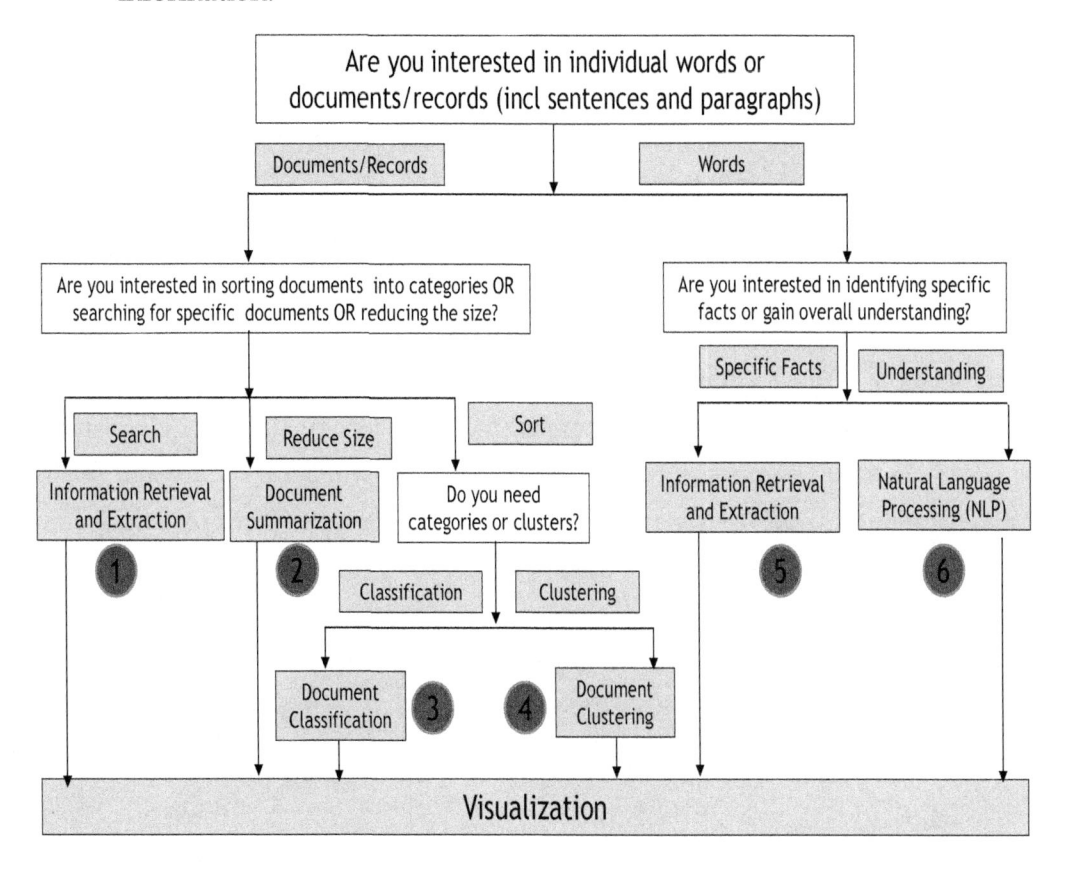

Figure 4.8: Six text analytics techniques

Balancing cost and business value in deriving analytics data type

The third capability deals with balancing the cost and business value in deriving analytics data types as realizing any best practice capability comes with the efficient utilization of business resources. In this backdrop, transforming the native data, especially the unstructured data to the analytics type of data, is a trade-off between the cost of data transformation to the analytics data type and the business value. While the continuous data type provides computational or statistical capabilities due to their inherent numeric features, they also demand a commitment of organizational resources.

Improving the data quality demands a thorough understanding of the company's products, services, customers, and the market the company is operating in.

To explain this concept, let us take a simple example in the supply chain where the delivery priority has options like urgent, priority, and standard. This delivery priority field is ordinal or ordered data where the urgent deliveries are delivered sooner than priority, and the priority deliveries are delivered sooner than the standard deliveries. If the ordinal data in the delivery type field is to be mapped and converted to continuous data, say one day for urgent orders, three days for priority orders, and seven days standard, it means there is a commitment on the resource utilization from the organization to deliver the goods to the customer within the stipulated or agreed time. While the continuous type of data gives options for statistical analysis, ultimately resulting in more objective and precise insights, it demands the commitment of the business resources to deliver those objective business outcomes.

Overall, transforming the data from the native state, especially the unstructured data format, to the analytics classification state (nominal, ordinal, and continuous) is balancing the business value of the insights derived to the cost of enabling business resources to provide that capability. This relationship is illustrated in Figure 4.9. The data transformation from native state to analytics state is not a purely technical endeavor; it is an exercise of business resource optimization. The best way to optimize business resources depends on the nature of the resources, that is, the decision variables, the business constraints at hand, and the organization's objectives. Technically, this means maximizing or minimizing, as appropriate, the performance objective by assigning values to the decision variables that satisfy the constraints. We will revisit this optimization topic again in chapter 8.

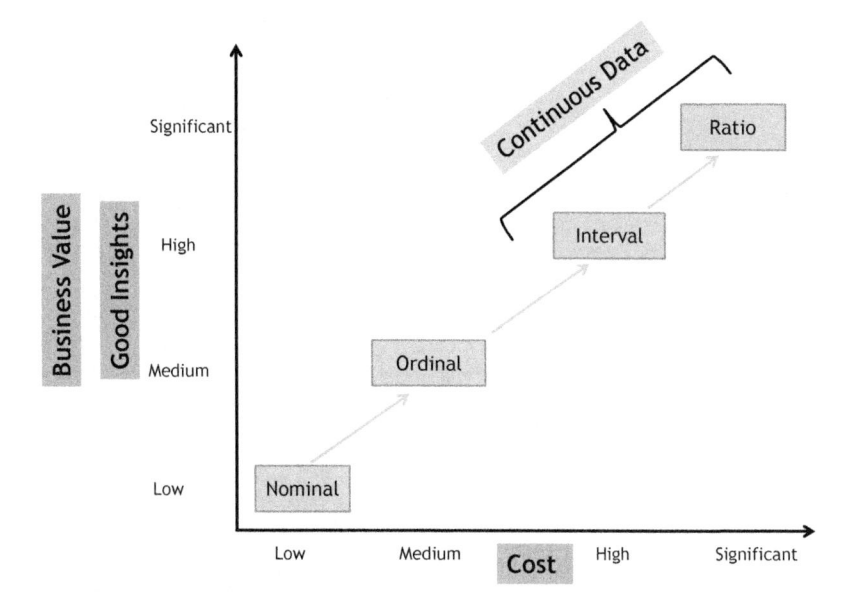

Figure 4.9: Balancing cost and business value

Conclusion

The origination of business data is mainly for compliance and operations, and in the process, the data is stored, integrated, and secured. However, this native state of data doesn't necessarily mean that the data is ready for analytics. If the data is needed for insights, then the data should be made available in an analytics format. While the analytics data types, that is, nominal, ordinal, and continuous data types, provide opportunities for statistical analytics and better insights, they also demand the commitment of the valuable resources of the organization. Business management is all about optimal utilization of the resources, and transforming the data to the analytics view demands different levels of resource consumption. Hence, if the business is looking at becoming a data-driven enterprise, data management, classification, and transformation to analytics view should be treated as a trade-off between cost and business value.

References

- Davis, Dwight, "AI Unleashes the Power of Unstructured Data," https://bit.ly/3bD9QkC, Jul 2019.
- Kimball, Ralph, "The Data Warehouse Lifecycle Toolkit," Wiley, 2008.
- Loshin, David, "Master Data Management," Morgan Kaufmann, 2009.
- Southekal, Prashanth, "Data for Business Performance," Technics Publications, 2017.

CHAPTER 5

Best Practice #4

Source Data for Analytics Strategically

"Strategy is about making choices and trade-off."
Michael Porter

One of the key elements for deriving good insights through analytics is quality data. However, many business enterprises are impacted by poor data quality that reduces productivity, creates inefficiencies, and increases operational costs. Recent Gartner research has found that poor data quality to be responsible for an average of US$ 15 million per year in losses in a company [Gartner, 2018]. The state of data quality is likely to worsen in the future for three main reasons:

1. IT systems are increasingly becoming large, complex, and disruptive and are altering the way consumers, industries, and businesses operate. This means diverse data models, data sources, and data definitions to manage.

2. Secondly, more companies are now diversifying with new products and services. Also, because of globalization, many companies are entering into new markets. This means more data on customers, suppliers, assets, and products, plus the transactional data on local regulations and business activities.

3. Thirdly, the mergers and acquisitions (M&A) market is consistently strong year-over-year across the globe. In 2017 there were 53,302 global

M&A deals, in 2018 it was 52,912 transactions, and in 2019 there were 49,849 M&A deals [Szmigiera, 2020]. This means more system consolidation and data integration in business enterprises, and data integration often results in poor data quality.

So, what exactly is data quality? There is no one universal definition of data quality. But from the business perspective, data quality is ensuring that the data is useful in business operations, compliance, and decision making [Southekal, 2017]. It is important to understand the key dimensions of data quality to define data quality comprehensively, as the definition of data quality is largely contextual. The word "dimension" is used to identify the key aspects of data that can be defined, quantified, implemented, and tracked. In this backdrop, there are 12 key dimensions of data quality, as shown in the figure on the facing page, and appendix 1 covers the definitions of these 12 data quality dimensions [Southekal, 2017].

Data quality doesn't mean that all the 12 data quality dimensions are applicable to a business all the time. Data quality is contextual, and often it is only the subset of these dimensions that matter to a business enterprise. Depending on the business problem, only a subset of these 12 attributes might be needed to assess the level of data quality.

So, as a fundamental question - why data quality is poor in business enterprises? Why are data analytics projects constrained with poor data quality? Why is considerable time and effort invested in data cleansing and remediation, technically known as data engineering? According to Armand Ruiz Gabernet of IBM, 80% of the time in analytics is spent on data engineering, leaving only 20% to derive insights [Gabernet, 2017].

Given that data quality is an essential requirement for analytics, there are five key reasons why data analytics is heavy on data engineering.

Figure 5.1: Data quality dimensions

1. **Different systems and technology mechanisms to integrate data.**
   Business systems are designed and implemented for a purpose, mainly for recording business transactions. The mechanisms for data capture in business systems such as ERP are batch or discrete data, while in the SCADA or IoT Field systems, it is for continuous or time-series data. This means that these business systems store diverse data types. Hence the technology (including the database itself) to capture data is varied and complex. When one is trying to integrate data from these diverse systems from different vendors, the metadata model varies, resulting in data integration challenges.

2. **Different time frames of data capture.** The timeframes for data ingestion into the IT systems during data capture varies. For example, in transactional applications like the ERP systems, data ingestion is typically batch, discrete, and manual, while in the field systems, data ingestion is usually automatic and near real-time. For example, when the product delivery to the customer is done, the shipment details are normally captured in real-time by the hand-held devices. But the invoicing cannot be immediately processed as invoices are issued from the ERP systems to the customer. This creates a delay in delivery-invoicing compliance reporting.

3. **Different user value-propositions.** In business, the same data is created and consumed by different stakeholders. This type of data is usually the internal business process data, and the value differs as the perspectives of the stakeholders vary. For example, while the technical attributes of an asset concern the engineering manager, the procurement manager looks at the purchasing aspects of the asset. This means for holistic asset analytics, the engineering data, and the purchasing data should be available.

4. **Different business processes.** The same data element can be different due to differences in business processes based on geographies, laws, regulations, market conditions, etc. For example, the date-of-birth data element of an employee in Canada is subject to data privacy regulations, while in many countries, the data privacy regulations are not very strong. So, getting the customer buying habit report based on age for a developing market is much easier than getting the same report in Canada.

5. **Different aggregations driven by organizational structures.** A data element can be viewed differently based on differences in granularities

or aggregations driven by organizational structures. For example, the VP of procurement might need a spend report based on item categories - an aggregation of items procured based on the item type, supplier type, delivery location, etc. But the procurement manager might need the spend report based on individual items procured, which are granular.

The different kinds of data engineering efforts and activities that make data engineering complex and an expensive process are illustrated below. In this backdrop, the phrase "real-time analytics," which is often used in the marketing materials of analytics consulting and product companies, is an oxymoron. This is because there is always a time lag between data origination and data capture. This time lag can be a few microseconds in SCADA/PoS systems, or this time lag might be even months before the data is formatted, cleansed, validated, curated, aggregated, and committed in a data warehouse before insights are derived. Inherently, data is historical, and hence the term "real-time analytics" is an oxymoron and doesn't exist. Instead, a better term for faster analytics can be *near real-time analytics*.

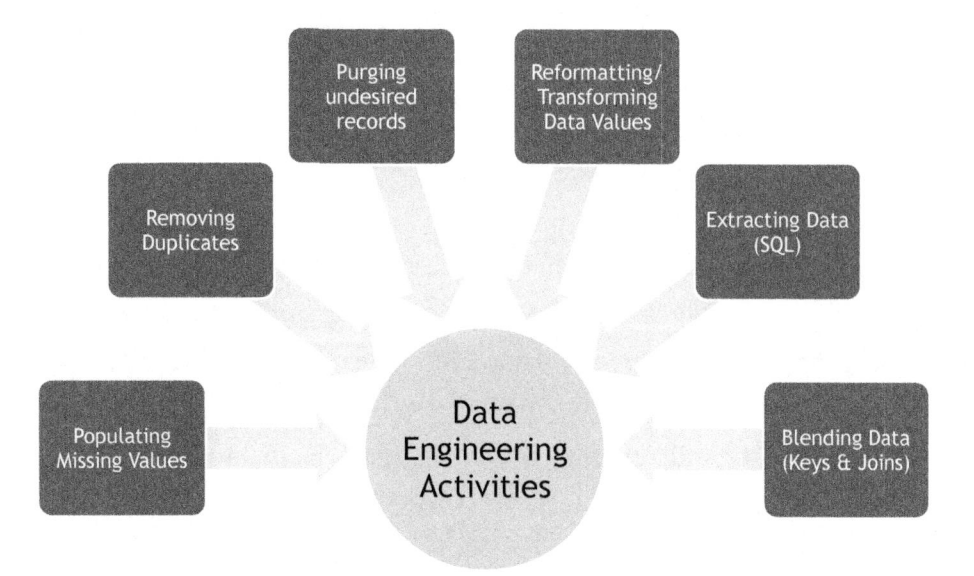

Figure 5.2: Data engineering activities

Why is this a best practice?

Why is strategically sourcing the data the best practice? Many analytics initiatives and managers assume that the data for analytics is readily and easily available in the enterprise. Unfortunately, businesses are plagued with poor quality data. As discussed earlier, most of the effort in analytics projects is on getting good quality data for deriving the insights. But from the data availability perceptive, analytics initiatives in business enterprises have two main challenges. First, there is no data at all. Second, there is no quality data. Below is some of the research done on the state of data quality in business enterprises.

- An average user spends two hours a day looking for the right data [Mckinsey, 2012]
- In 2016, a study by IBM concluded that bad data cost the US economy US$ 3.1 trillion [Ross, 2019].
- Up to 73% of data in an organization is never used for analytics [Forrester, 2016]

> A business enterprise is an evolving entity; it is subject to changes all the time.
>
> Without a continuous program of measuring and monitoring, data quality will degrade over time.

Despite poor-quality data in the enterprise, appropriate data acquisition strategies should be derived so that business can go forward in deriving good insights. Fundamentally as the business environment evolves, organizations also adapt to the evolving environment. Given the flux in the operating environment of the business, the business model is never stable. Hence, the performance and the utilization of the business assets, including data, are rarely in the ideal or stable or perfect state.

So, what is the approach? They say perfection is the opposite of getting things done. Voltaire, the French writer, said, "The best is the enemy of the good."

George Patton, the American WWII general, had said – "A good plan today is better than a perfect plan tomorrow." Focusing on perfection or getting high-quality data becomes a productivity problem. It can lead to a feeling of paralysis, of being stuck in the task in which one can never get the desired result. The bottom line is that in the current business paradigm or model, there is no state like perfect high-quality data that can be used in business analytics. Businesses must find some alternatives to get the best available data.

Realizing the best practice

Given that getting quality data is a huge challenge in analytics initiatives, how can businesses get good data for deriving meaningful insights? What are the alternatives to get the best available data? The trick is to stay focused on the final product and not put too much emphasis on the process. So, what is the final product in analytics? It is insights and not data per se; data is the vehicle to get good insights. Businesses essentially need good reliable insights.

In chapter 1 we saw that insights could come from intuition as well, apart from data. Also, as discussed in chapter 1 in the last mile analytics (LMA) section, even though data is the foundation for analytics, data collection is practically a non-value-added task for the business. It is an inevitable process; we can only aspire to shorten this process, but we cannot eliminate it. How can we shorten this data collection activity and focus on deriving and implementing the insights? Overall, data is expensive to manage; the value of getting insights should be significantly higher than the cost of generating insights.

In addition, many business processes do not need high-quality data. For example, accurate data is good enough compared to correct data, and there is a big effort required in moving to the correct data state from accurate data state; accuracy and correctness are two of the 12 data quality dimensions. For example, if a Telecom company's primary channel to reach its customer is the customer's phone number, then the phone number should be correct, and the home address can be accurate. Fixing home addresses when people move places would be expensive and even unnecessary for the Telecom company if the primary contact mode is via the telephone. The Telecom company can save time and costs if it keeps the home address as accurate and phone number as correct, instead of having both the home address and phone number as correct.

So, what are the options to get good data for analytics? There are three main workaround strategies or options the business enterprises can leverage to overcome this challenge of poor data quality. These three strategies will help the business in deriving insights quickly and implementing them for business efficiencies.

1. Data sampling
2. Feature engineering (FE)
3. Acquiring and blending data

A key pre-requisite for implementing these three workaround strategies is a strong knowledge of the business and the associated processes. In addition, the data derived from applying these three workaround strategies should be validated against the 12 data quality dimensions discussed earlier.

Data sampling

Data sampling is selecting a representative subset of data from a larger population of data. The goal is to work with a small amount of data that is reflecting the characteristics of the actual population. Data sampling will help one derive insights quickly and cost-effectively as only a small data set is prepared for deriving insights. But there are two important considerations in acquiring a good data sample are:

1. the **size** of the required data sample and
2. the possibility of the **sampling error** in the selected data sample

To address the first issue on the sample data size or count, sample data size or data count should be based on three main factors:

1. Population in question. This factor is on the total size of the population in question. For example, if the data analytics is on procurement spend for the last three years, then the total count of purchase orders issued by the company is needed. The count of purchase orders can be easily retrieved from the ERP or Procurement systems in the company.
2. The margin of error (MoE). MoE is the percentage that expresses the probability that the data collected is accurate, and MoE is typically fixed at 5%.
3. Confidence level (CL). It is the probability that the MoE is accurate, and CL is generally set at 95%.

These three variables, population, MoE, and CL, can be used in a statistical formula to get the sample size or count, or there are many online tools that can help one to get the sample size easily. The image below is the sample count of 384 purchase orders coming out from an online tool called SurveyMonkey after analyzing the population of 839,997 purchase orders at 5% MoE and at a 95% confidence level.

Once the sample count is determined, we need to ensure that the sample size or count is not subject to **sampling error**. Sampling error, which is the second issue in data sampling, is the situation where the sample selected is not the true representation of the population. Sampling errors can be eliminated by ensuring that the sample size adequately **represents** the entire population, and the samples are **randomly** selected. The randomness in the selected data, can be validated with tests such as the runs test. Technically, runs test is used to test the hypothesis that the elements of the data set are mutually independent.

Calculate your sample size

Population size	Confidence level (%)	Margin of error (%)
839,997	95	5

Sample size

384

Figure 5.3: Sampling count in SurveyMonkey

In other words, representation of the population and randomization in the data selection are two key factors to minimize sampling error. In the above example, if the 384 sample purchase orders selected are from one geography for one item category from one vendor, it does not reflect the true nature of the entire population of 839,997 purchase orders especially if the company operates in multiple countries and procures items from multiple vendors from different item categories. To summarize, sample data should be of good count, should be randomly selected, and should represent the characteristics of the actual population well. The relationship is illustrated on the facing page.

When the sample data selected has addressed risks on sample count and sampling error, you must make sure that the insights derived from the sample data are not likely by chance. Statistical significance expressed as p-value helps to quantify whether the insight gleaned from sample data is due to chance. The lower the p-value (lower than 0.05), the less likely that the results are due to chance, technically known as rejecting the null hypothesis. For example, a t-test, one of the important statistical tests, tells if the difference in means between two sample data sets is significant or if the difference in means could have happened by chance. If the p-value in the t-test output is less than 0.05, we reject the null hypothesis and conclude that there is a difference between the two sample data sets if it were extended to the entire population. Similarly, in the regression output that uses sample data, a low p-value means that the data variable can be included in the regression model and would work for the population data set during predictive analytics.

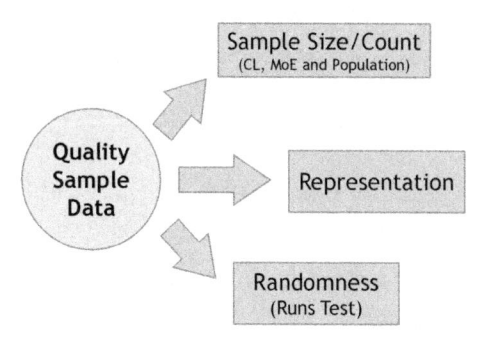

Figure 5.4: Data sampling

Feature engineering

The second strategy to get good data for analytics quickly is feature engineering. Fundamentally analytics algorithms take data as the input to give the insights as to the output. But getting good quality data in the right data format to be used as an input to the algorithms is a challenge in most business enterprises. This is where feature engineering addresses the problem. Feature engineering is creating a "smarter" dataset or attributes or features applying the domain experience and intuition on the existing data sets. Feature engineering serves two main purposes:

- Transform data types
- Create new fields or attributes.

With feature engineering, the integrity of the data is never compromised.

Let us first discuss how feature engineering can be used to transform data types using an example. In multiple linear regression (MLR) algorithms, the output or dependent variable is in numeric format, and the input or independent variable is in continuous format. But if the input or the independent variables are in the nominal format, one option is to use dummy variables in the MLR, and the second option is to transform the nominal variable into a continuous variable using feature engineering. For example, in a retail chain, if the store area field has values large, medium, and small, the nominal field can be converted to numeric by assigning a value of 5 to large, 3 to medium, and 1 to small.

The second function of feature engineering is creating new fields. Often, data in many business operations are repeated across datasets, and this data can be used to build or derive new data attributes or features. Below is a sample where the initial or original production data from the factory floor can be used to derive new attributes or features without compromising the underlying data integrity. In Figure 5.5, based on the timestamp, a new field or attribute called "shift" is derived. If the timestamp field has a value between 13 to 15 hours, then the shift is "Day," if the timestamp has a value of 16 hours, then the shift is "Break," and if the timestamp has a value between 17 to 19 hours, then the shift is "Night."

Acquiring and blending data

The third option or the best practice for companies to get good quality data for analytics quickly is to acquire new datasets and blend it with an existing dataset to make it into a functioning dataset. This happens when the company lacks key data attributes in its dataset to do analytics – especially predictive and prescriptive analytics. While descriptive analytics primarily deals with historical data, predictive and prescriptive analytics will typically rely on a combination of historical datasets and new datasets. There are three key steps in this approach of acquiring new data and blending it with existing data:

Original Data				Transformed Data				
Quantity	TimeStamp	Product Id		Quantity	Weekday	Hour	Category	Shift
52	2019-05-04 13:00	80818579		52	4	1	Bearing	Day
56	2019-05-04 14:00	86858562		56	4	2	Flanges	Day
54	2019-05-04 15:00	80878581		54	4	3	Coupling	Day
20	2019-05-04 16:00	80818569		20	4	4	Bearing	Break
55	2019-05-04 17:00	80818566		55	4	5	Bearing	Night
54	2019-05-04 18:00	80818579		54	4	6	Bearing	Night
57	2019-05-04 19:00	86858562		57	4	7	Flanges	Night
52	2019-05-05 13:00	80878581		52	5	1	Coupling	Day
56	2019-05-05 14:00	80818569		56	5	2	Bearing	Day
54	2019-05-05 15:00	80818566		54	5	3	Bearing	Day
21	2019-05-05 16:00	80818566		20	5	4	Bearing	Break
54	2019-05-05 17:00	80818579		55	5	5	Bearing	Night
54	2019-05-05 18:00	86858562		54	5	6	Flanges	Night
56	2019-05-05 19:00	80878581		57	5	7	Coupling	Night

Figure 5.5: Feature engineering

Data acquisition

New business data could be acquired internally or externally. Internally new dataset could come in three main ways - business experiments, PoC (Proof-of-concept), and surveys.

1. A business experiment is applying tools and techniques on different hypotheses and acquiring new data.

2. A PoC (Proof of Concept) is a small and quick exercise to verify and validate the functionality. A PoC is usually a small exercise to test the design idea or assumption and, in the process, acquire new data.

3. A survey is a research method used for collecting data from a pre-defined group of respondents to gain insights on a specific topic of interest.

> *A business experiment should always begin with the definition of what constitutes a valid testable hypothesis.*

Externally the new datasets could be acquired from sources such as Kaggle (https://www.kaggle.com/datasets), Google (https://cloud.google.com/public-datasets/). Microsoft (https://msropendata.com/), Government-published datasets from EU, US, India, and Canada, for example. These datasets are normally available for free as Open data. Also, datasets can be purchased from external companies like Bloomberg, IHS-Markit, Statista, Snowflake cloud data warehouse, and others for a nominal fee. Below is the Snowflake's Data Exchange marketplace that utilizes secure data sharing to connect data providers with data consumers.

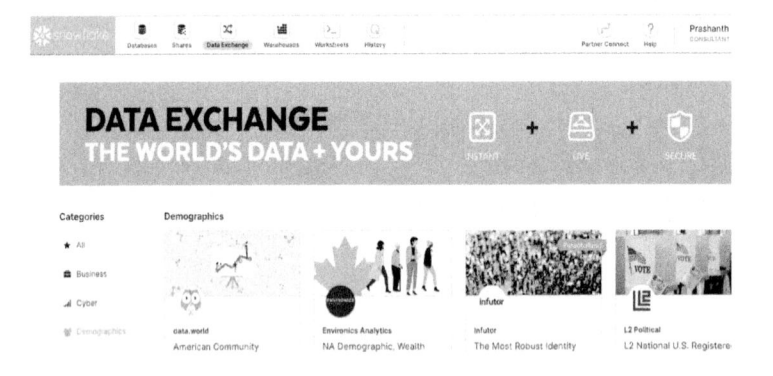

Figure 5.6: Data exchange in Snowflake

Combining data with joins and unions

Once the datasets are acquired – internally or externally, the data can be combined with the available or existing dataset to form an integrated dataset. Two key SQL operations to combine datasets are JOINS AND UNIONS. A (SQL) JOIN combines columns from one or more database tables using the primary keys (PK) and foreign keys (FK). The PK uniquely identifies a record in the table, while the FK is a field in the table that is PK in another table. A foreign key, by contrast, is one or more fields or columns that correspond to the primary key of another table. Foreign keys are what make it possible to join tables with each other. Closely related to JOIN is the UNION operation. If two tables with similar data structures are combined using the UNION operation, then the data from the first table is in one set of rows, and the data from the second table in another set. The rows are in the same result. In simple terms, JOIN combines data into new columns, and UNION combines data into new rows.

Data cleansing

Once the data is combined to form an integrated data set, the integrated dataset should be cleansed to form a usable or functional dataset so that data scientists can use it in analytics for deriving insights. Data cleansing on the integrated dataset at this stage involves four main activities:

- Populating any missing values
- Standardizing and enriching the integrated data.
- Removing duplicate records if any
- Validating and verifying the data with key business stakeholders

Conclusion

Data is the fuel for running analytics algorithms or models. But getting good quality data for analytics is challenging for most business enterprises. A study from the Harvard Business Review discovered that data quality is far worse than most companies realize, saying that a mere 3% of the data quality scores in the study were rated as "acceptable" [Nagle et al., 2017]. So, should the analytic initiatives wait for the data quality to improve, or is there a workaround?

There are many options or workarounds for getting good quality like data sampling, feature engineering, and acquiring and blending new data from internal or external sources. The analytics team should strategically source data given that getting perfect high-quality data is nearly impossible in most scenarios. However, if quality population data is available, it is always recommended to use the population dataset. These three strategies, however, do not fix the data quality problem in the company; they are essentially best practice workarounds that allow one to move forward with your analytics initiatives. As civil rights movement leader, Martin Luther King Jr said, "If you can't fly then run, if you can't run then walk, if you can't walk then crawl, but whatever you do you have to keep moving forward." And according to tennis player, Arthur Ashe, "Start where you are. Use what you have. Do what you can."

References

- Forrester, https://bit.ly/2USU9ij, Jan 2016.
- Gabernet, Armand Ruiz, "Breaking the 80/20 rule: How data catalogs transform data scientists' productivity," https://ibm.co/2yiqbwE, 2017.
- Gartner, "How to Create a Business Case for Data Quality Improvement," https://gtnr.it/345AJLt, Jun 2018.
- Mckinsey, "The social economy: Unlocking value and productivity through social technologies," July 2012.
- Nagle, Tadhg; Redman, Thomas, and David Sammon, "Only 3% of Companies' Data Meets Basic Quality Standards," https://bit.ly/2UxaHO4, Sep 2017.
- Ross, Andrew, "Experian study: why organisations think they have bad data," https://bit.ly/2w3th79, Feb 2019.
- Szmigiera, M, "Number of merger and acquisition transactions worldwide from 1985 to 2019," https://bit.ly/2xGXpFy, Feb 2020.

CHAPTER 6

Best Practice #5

Make Data Compliance an Integral Part of Analytics

"It takes 20 years to build a reputation and 5 minutes to ruin it. If you think about that, you will do things differently."

Warren Buffet

As data becomes the new currency of the world, new rules are drawn on business data analytics, and one of the key rules is on data compliance. What exactly is data compliance, and how does it impact data analytics? In simple words, data compliance is the adherence of data on four key aspects:

1. **Government Laws and Regulations**. A law is a rule of conduct developed by the government or society over a certain jurisdiction. Regulations, on the other hand, are rules adopted by the government agencies that govern how laws will be enforced.

2. **Internal Business Rules.** Business rules are statements that give businesses the criteria and conditions for making decisions. Business rules provide businesses the structure to control or influence the operation of the business.

3. **Industry Standards.** Industry standards are a set of criteria within an industry related to the functioning of the business entity within the

industry. In other words, industry standards are the generally accepted practices followed by the member companies of the industry sector. For example, due to the global nature of the automotive industry, there are numerous communications and document standards used, such as ANSI (American National Standards Institute) and EDIFACT (Electronic Data Interchange for Administration, Commerce, and Transport) used by the businesses in the automotive industry.

4. **Ethics.** Business ethics are a set of moral rules that govern how businesses operate. Data ethics, which are driven by business ethics, prescribes what business ought to do with data in terms of rights, obligations, impact to society, or fairness in business operations.

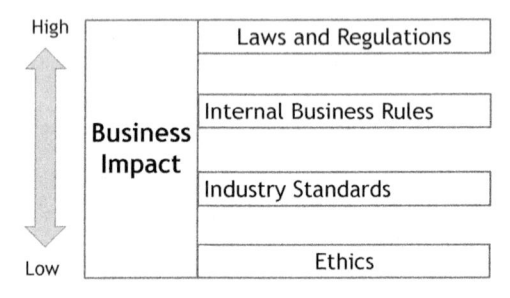

Figure 6.1: Data compliance considerations

Why is this a best practice?

Data compliance is compliance to government laws and regulations, to industry standards, to business rules, and to ethics. What is the business impact on each of these four elements on data compliance?

1. Failure to comply with data compliance laws and regulations can have serious consequences for both individuals and organizations, including fines, imprisonment, and disqualification. In 2019, France's DPA (Data

Protection Authorities) imposed 50 million euros as fine against Google for failing to properly disclose to users how data is collected across services [Dunn, 2019].

2. Non-compliance of data to industry standards will result in products and services produced not being safe and reliable for consumption. For instance, standards on road safety and secure medical packaging rely on compliance with ISO standards.

3. Non-compliance of data to internal business rules will affect the business productivity of the company.

4. Finally, not being ethical in conducting business operations will affect the brand and the reputation of the company.

In addition, while data can be an asset, it can even be a liability when not complied with laws, internal business rules, industry standards, and ethics. There are three situations where data can be a liability to the business.

- Firstly, collecting data without a defined purpose will result in data management complexity, increased cost, and missed business opportunities. According to Forrester, 73% of data in a company is never used strategically [Forrester, 2016]. While the time and effort to acquire, secure, and store this data is significant, the opportunity cost of not utilizing this data in today's digital world is massive.

- Secondly, data takes up a vast amount of energy to store, secure, and process, and this costs money to the business and increases its carbon footprint. According to Deloitte, the average IT spending across industries is 3.28% of the revenue, and it grows at an average of 49% every year [Deloitte, 2018]. Apart from the financial costs, the amount of energy used by data centers continues to double every four years, affecting the carbon footprint. In 2018, data centers consumed about 1.1% of total global electricity. By 2025, the energy consumption of data centers is set to account for 3.2% of the total worldwide carbon emissions consuming 20% of global electricity [Trueman, 2019].

- Thirdly, with the rise of cybercrime and data breaches these days, companies are faced with the task of securely ensuring the safety of data. Apart from major data breaches, collecting and using data is also a potential privacy and legal liability. In general, people don't like to be spied on. For example, when consumers receive unsolicited promotional materials, it can be annoying and might even damage the relationship the consumers have with the company.

Too much of a good thing can sometimes be a bad thing; while data can be a great business asset, it can quickly become a huge liability for the business. Figure 6.2 shows the amount of quality data in the business and its impact on the actual performance of the business. The bottom line is that data can be a business asset only if it is within a specific range. While little data impairs data-driven business performance, lots of data can also hamper business operations. The bottom line is that if the business data does not follow compliance requirements, the business can have a massive financial loss, inefficient business operations, and irreparable damage to its reputation. This can ultimately affect the existence of the firm. Hence the data analytics team should look at compliance elements like compliance to laws and regulations, compliance to industry standards and business rules, and compliance to ethical aspects, as an integral part of business analytics. Take, for example, Nexen, an oil company based in Alberta, Canada. When Nexen spilled over 30,000 barrels of crude oil in July of 2015 in Alberta, Canada, the Alberta Energy Regulator (AER) ordered the immediate suspension of 15 pipeline licenses issued to Nexen due to lack of maintenance data records. This is an example of a lack of compliance data to the regulations set by the provincial energy regulator.

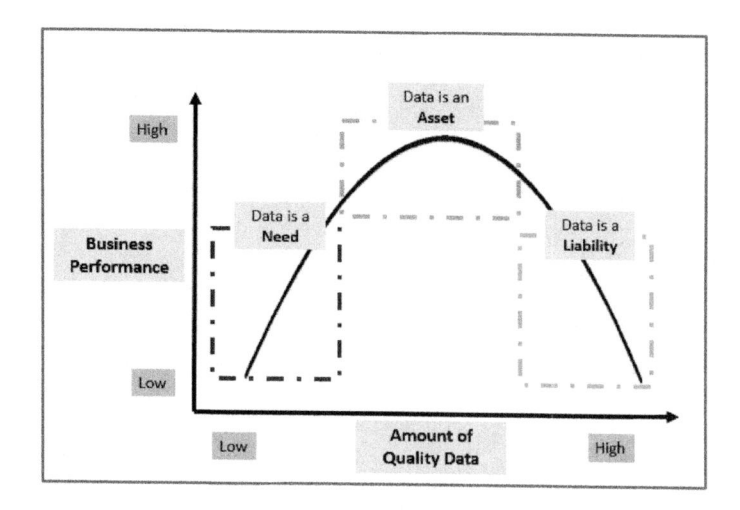

Figure 6.2: Amount of data V/s business impact

In 2017, hackers accessed hundreds of millions of customer records from the credit reporting agency, Equifax. This is an example of a lack of compliance with the security standards, that is, internal business rules, as the company spent US$1.4 billion to transform the technology infrastructure. The Facebook–Cambridge Analytica data scandal resulted in Facebook losing US$35 billion in market value following reports that Cambridge Analytica had unauthorized access to over 50 million Facebook user accounts. This is an example of a lack of compliance with the privacy regulations and data ethics from both Facebook and Cambridge Analytica.

Data Management is all about balance! Plan and then execute. Don't rush!

Realizing the best practice

How can businesses ensure compliance to data? At the highest level, data compliance is the responsible and sustainable use of data. While no or little data in the business is a problem for business, often lot of data is also a problem if compliance aspects are not managed properly. The scale, pace, and ease with which analytics can be conducted today completely change the compliance framework on data management. In this regard, data considerations for analytics compliance can happen by addressing three main capabilities:

1. Compliance to external and internal mandates
2. Compliance to purpose
3. Compliance to transparency

Compliance to external and internal mandates

If companies must operate in a jurisdiction, they must follow the applicable laws and regulations, that is, external mandates. Compliance with external mandates is adhering to laws on privacy, payments, environment, and other government regulations. Data privacy concerns with the proper handling of personally identifiable information (PII) data with consent, notice, and regulatory obligations. If the business collects payments from credit cards, then the business must adhere to the Payment Card Industry Data Security Standard (PCI DSS). The US Environmental Protection Agency (EPA) has standards for reducing greenhouse gas emissions, and oil companies are mandated to follow these EPA guidelines. The Sarbanes-Oxley (SOX) Act is to protect investors from fraudulent financial reporting, and businesses must present financial reports in adherence to SOX Act.

The compliance to internal mandates is mainly on data security, that is, ensuring that business activities are conducted securely. Data security needs to be applied across multiple layers on both during Data in Motion (DIM) and Data at Rest (DAR). This starts with understanding the flow of data, that is, data lineage or data provenance, and classifying data based on its sensitivity, that is, restricted, confidential, or open. And if the data is sensitive, one must then look at data protection measures such as role-based access control (RBAC), authorization management, encryption, network security, and database protection, to name a few.

> *The right level of data compliance balances business risk with agility.*

Compliance to purpose

While companies have an option or flexibility in managing internal operational business processes and the associated data in their own way, they have little or no option on capturing regulatory data. Collect only what is mandated when capturing regulatory data. For example, when collecting privacy-related data, businesses should only collect what is needed. If the person's date of birth is not needed, then businesses should not collect it. This helps in not only holding sensitive data but also saves the company with the bandwidth in protecting that data. Fundamentally, while data is an asset, it can be a liability as well as seen in the data breach cases of Equifax, CapitalOne, Cambridge Analytica, Marriott Hotels, Target, and many more.

A key technique to ensure that the data captured is purpose-driven is by ensuring that the data elements on business categories, entities, and events are mapped to every element on the business value stream map (VSM). A VSM is a visual tool that shows the flow of materials and data the company uses to produce a product or service for its customers. VSM has its origins to lean manufacturing, and the business value of VSM is to identify and remove or reduce waste in the process, thereby increasing the efficiency in the system.

The key to developing a strong VSM is to treat your business as a network (of customers, employees, vendors, dealers, partners, and so on.) and not as an aggregation of individual LoBs. This means looking at the entire value chain on how the firm's products and services reach the end consumers. Put simply, looking at VSM as a business network will improve the management of expenses, enable inventory control, better information flow, and will optimize the company's cash flow and growth. As Aristotle said – "The whole is greater than the sum of its parts." and this is very much relevant in developing VSMs.

So, if the data element in question is not finding a place in the value stream map (VSM), that means the data element potentially has no business value and shouldn't be captured and stored. Below is a simple example of VSM in an oil company, where the key data elements are mapped to the individual value streams.

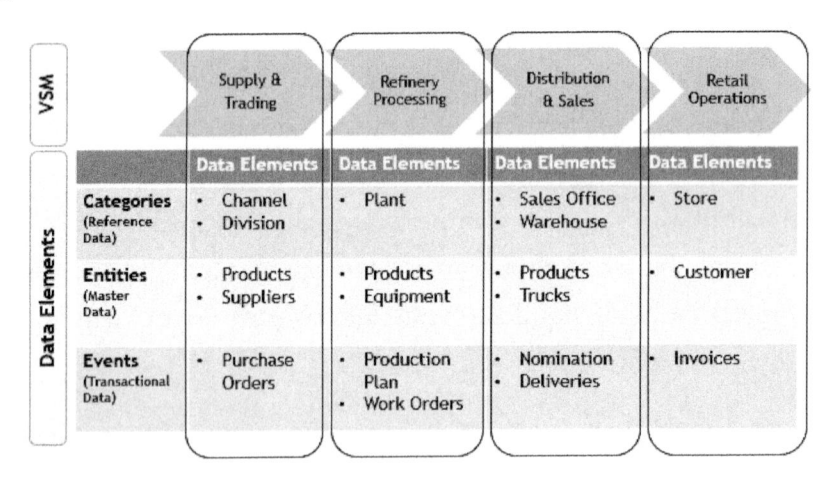

		Supply & Trading	Refinery Processing	Distribution & Sales	Retail Operations
		Data Elements	**Data Elements**	**Data Elements**	**Data Elements**
	Categories (Reference Data)	• Channel • Division	• Plant	• Sales Office • Warehouse	• Store
	Entities (Master Data)	• Products • Suppliers	• Products • Equipment	• Products • Trucks	• Customer
	Events (Transactional Data)	• Purchase Orders	• Production Plan • Work Orders	• Nomination • Deliveries	• Invoices

Figure 6.3: VSM-Data elements mapping

While the consumption of restricted data in the business is defined by laws and regulations, the purpose or consumption of confidential data or internal business data is normally defined by business rules. For example, vendor purchase order data might be of interest both to the finance department and the purchasing department. In that case, purchase order data authorization should be done at the point of data capture so that the right users are authorized to access the right data based on their role. This role-to-position (RTP) authorization ensures data integrity along with offering non-repudiation and traceability features to data.

Compliance to transparency

Transparency in the context of data compliance is building education and awareness on handling data in business operations. Business stakeholders should have a clear understanding of how the business data is extracted, migrated, and transformed, the way data lineage exists across systems. Data lineage is tracking data from the point of origination until it is archived or purged. Transparency is also on the way the data and insights are shared with the business stakeholders. For example, privacy data does not mean secrecy, and that data should not be shared. Privacy data that is obtained from the person can be shared with their consent. Similarly, sensitive data —asset, financial data, or locational data—need to have restrictions on when and how that data can be shared. However, the aggregate data used in BI (Business Intelligence) systems can have a broad level of access, but granular data that is captured and stored in the transactional systems should be mapped to the right business roles and positions.

Implementation of data compliance to data transparency is typically done with Digital Asset Management (DAM) systems, which help in organizing, storing, and retrieving digital assets (structured and unstructured data) with the appropriate rights and permissions. Technically, DAM holds metadata records that contain the name of the file, its format, and details about its content and usage from a central content hub. In simple words, DAM is a digital library of all the digital assets of the enterprise – documentation, images, audio, video, presentations, podcasts, animations, and any other digital content – in an easy-to-access, quick-to-search, centralized location.

Conclusion

Even though data is a business asset and a key component in analytics, the compliance aspects, if not managed well, can limit the use of data in analytics. Data analytics can be adversely impacted by compliance issues, especially when dealing with data related to laws and regulations and when companies begin using their data for purposes different from those for which the data was initially collected. The bottom line is that data compliance is an integral part of analytics, and compliance aspects should be addressed with the right stakeholders having access to the right data and insights. It should be addressed upfront immediately when the stakeholder needs are identified, and the data is selected, not after insights are derived and about to be consumed. Last but not least, data compliance should be driven by the business sponsor for the analytics programs and should be one of the key charters for the Chief Data Officer (CDO). In short, data is an asset only if managed well. If not, it can become a liability or even a nightmare.

References

- Deloitte, "IT Spending: From Value Preservation to Value Creation" https://bit.ly/3bF3jWv, Mar 2018.
- Forrester, https://bit.ly/3axJ50V, Jan 2016.
- Gibson Dunn, "The French Data Protection Authority Imposes a 50 Million Euros Fine on Google LLC," https://bit.ly/2WUk3Ff, Jan 2019.
- Southekal, Prashanth, "Data for Business Performance," Technics Publications, 2017.
- Trueman, Charlotte, "Why data centres are the new frontier in the fight against climate change," https://bit.ly/2X4jzMZ, Aug 2019.

CHAPTER 7

Best Practice #6

Focus on Descriptive Analytics for Data Literacy

> *"Over 85% of Data Analytics in the Industry is Descriptive Analytics."*
>
> *Gartner*

As discussed in the preceding sections, businesses today originate and capture enormous amounts of data. But many companies struggle to become a data-driven enterprise. Research published in Harvard Business Review found that companies are failing in their efforts to become data-driven and the percentage of firms identifying themselves as being data-driven has declined in each of the past three years – from 37.1% in 2017 to 32.4% in 2018 to 31.0% in 2019 [Bean and Davenport, 2019]. Some alarming results from the research are:

- 72% of survey participants report that they have yet to forge a data culture
- 69% report that they have not created a data-driven organization
- 53% state that they are not yet treating data as a business asset
- 52% admit that they are not competing on data and analytics.

One of the main reasons that prevent companies from becoming data-driven is the lack of data literacy, which is the ability to understand and communicate data and insights. In fact, according to Gartner, data literacy is the second key reason that is preventing companies to become data-driven and by 2020, 50% of organizations will lack sufficient AI and data literacy skills to achieve business value [Gartner, 2019]. The key findings of Gartner's CDO research are below.

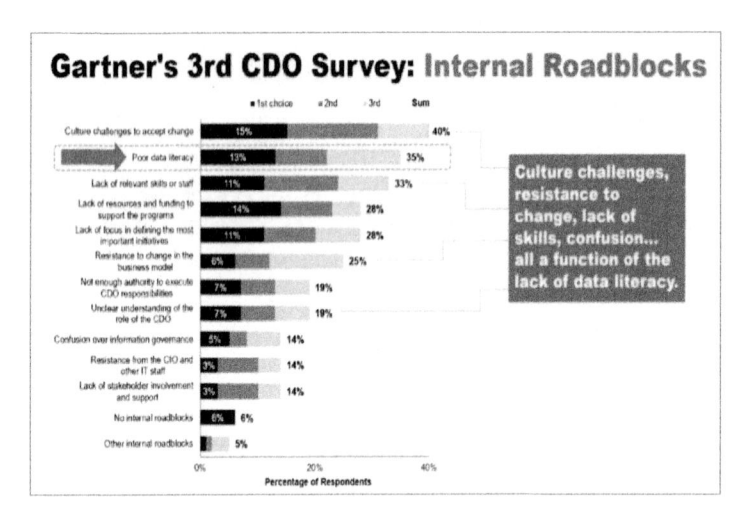

Figure 7.1: Gartner's CDO research

So, how can data literacy be inculcated in the business enterprise? While there are many strategies to drive data literacy and one key strategy is leveraging the execution of descriptive analytics. But what exactly is descriptive analytics in the context of data literacy? Descriptive analytics is interpreting historical data to better understand past business performance. In simple words, descriptive analytics answers the question, "what happened?" using historical business data. Examples include, what were our sales last quarter? Who are the top five vendors based on dollar spend? Which product had the most defects? Questions like these form the foundation for the entire analytics strategy as these types of basic questions and the associated key performance indicators (KPIs) form the basis of enterprise business performance.

Descriptive analytics is the most common of the three types of analytics in business: the other two being predictive and prescriptive analytics. According to business analytics experts, Piyanka Jain and Puneet Sharma, 80% of the analytics reports used in enterprises are descriptive in nature [Jain and Sharma, 2014].

According to Gartner, just 13% of organizations are using predictive, and 3% are using prescriptive reports; just 16% of the reports are on advanced analytics; a combination of predictive and prescriptive analytics [Williamson, 2015].

> *A holistic analytics solution should address the insight needs of analysts, managers, and executives.*

Descriptive analytics is technically realized with dashboards and reports using the MAD (Monitor-Analyze-Detail) framework, which is explained below.

- **Monitor.** The monitor type of insights is the dashboard' part of descriptive analytics. A business dashboard is not much different from the dashboard in a car. It visually conveys a quick snapshot of the required information or KPIs.

- **Analysis.** The analysis level provides the ability to dig a little deeper to understand the issue. For example, when using the sales reports, one can get details on sales managers, products, stores, and customers. The descriptive analytics in this category will typically have charts and KPIs at an aggregated and multi-dimensional level. In other words, it is mostly the BI reports.

- **Detail.** Once the information is drilled in, further details may be needed. For example, one sales area's margin might be much lower on average than other regions, and one might want to view all the details of pertinent transactions. The descriptive analytics here is often the reports coming directly from the transactional systems.

Within the MAD framework, the monitor function is for the senior management, the analysis function is mainly for the managers, and the detail function is for the analysts. The MAD Insight consumption framework is in Figure 7.2.

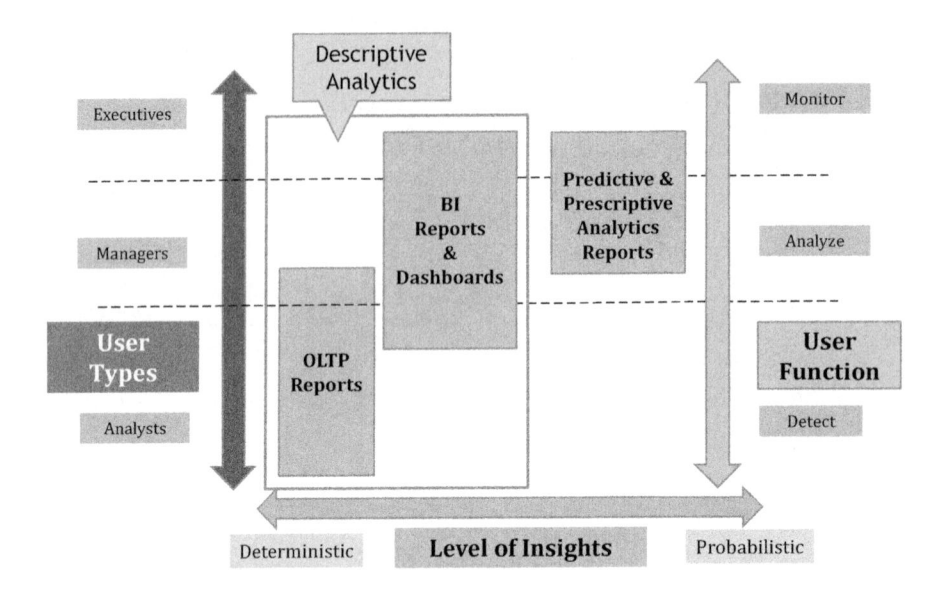

Figure 7.2: MAD Framework

The table below contains the mapping of the MAD framework to the user type and the three types of analytics.

Analytics Types	Monitor	Analyze	Detect
Descriptive Analytics – Transactional Reports	Executives and Managers	Analyst and Managers	Analyst
Descriptive Analytics – BI Reports	Executives and Managers	Managers	Analyst
Predictive Analytics	Executives and Managers	Managers	Managers
Prescriptive Analytics	Executives and Managers	Managers	Managers

Why is this a best practice?

So, how can descriptive analytics help with data literacy in the business? As discussed earlier, data literacy is enabling the business stakeholders to work with both data and insights for better business performance. So, if organizations can get reliable, quick, and easy access to both data and the insights and if they practice and work in that insights-based environment long enough, then data literacy can be potentially achieved. According to an article in HBR, it takes time and deliberate practice to become an expert [Ericsson et al., 2007]. According to the American Educator Edgar Dale, who developed the *Cone of Experience* or the *Learning Pyramid*, the more experiential is the learning, the greater is the retention by the individual of what they are learning. Malcolm Gladwell, in his bestselling book, *Outliers*, said one needs 10,000 hours of practice to gain expertise. The general premise is - systematic and constant exposure to data, and the insights will enhance data literacy in the organization, and descriptive analytics can offer that promise.

But how does descriptive analytics offer that promise? While data and insights can be provided by one of the three types of analytics – descriptive, predictive, and prescriptive, why is descriptive analytics preferred over others? The reason is descriptive analytics facilitates reliable, quick, and easy access to data and insights. There are five main reasons for this.

1. **Predictability**. The data and insights in descriptive analytics are deterministic and factual. For example, the sales figures for the year 2018 are the same for everyone in the company; it is a fact coming from a descriptive analytics report. On the other hand, insights from the predictive analytics model bring uncertainty. For instance, in the regression model, an R-square value of 0.82 and a p-value of 0.0023 though statistically acceptable, might be unacceptable to a person if he or she has a low-risk appetite.

2. **Consistency**. As there will be a single and consistent version of insights derived in descriptive analytics, the communication of the insights to the stakeholders becomes simpler. If the business can understand the insight or KPI well, the problem of transforming the insight into actions is much

bigger. So, fundamentally, the insights or KPIs presented in descriptive analytics (reports and dashboards), can be the vehicle for communication to help build data literacy in the company.

3. **Reduced cost**. The data used for deriving insights in descriptive analytics is easily and readily available in IT systems as the data is recorded on the past business events or transactions. This improves the speed of data acquisition, thereby reducing cost.

4. **Quicker insights**. The capability or the technology to deliver insights in descriptive analytics is simple and fast compared to the insights derived using predictive and prescriptive analytics. The reports and dashboards in descriptive analytics are typically out-of-the-box solutions in most transactional and BI systems. In predictive and prescriptive analytics, there is uncertainty in the algorithm selected, the data used, and even the insights that are derived are probabilistic.

5. **Roadmap**. Lastly, data literacy is also needed for advanced analytics, that is, predictive and prescriptive analytics. Descriptive analytics helps in assessing the current analytics maturity and identifies the gaps for the company to move up the analytics maturity curve or the analytics value chain. In other words, understanding the analytics maturity in the organization will help in preparing the roadmap for predictive and prescriptive analytics.

Research by IBM says that basic reporting and dashboarding capabilities, that is, descriptive analytics capabilities, can improve the return on investment (ROI) by 188%, and improving data quality can further boost the ROI to as high as 1209% [IBM, 2017]. For all these reasons, descriptive analytics can be a key enabler for building data literacy in the company.

Realizing the best practice

So, how can a business enterprise use descriptive analytics for data literacy? To implement descriptive analytics and build data literacy, a business enterprise must harness three key capabilities:

1. Use data to build the data-driven culture
2. Building data pipelines
3. Implementing reports and dashboards

Use data to build the data-driven culture

The foundation for data literacy is a data-driven culture. Organizations need to promote a data-first culture that encourages data-driven decision making (3DM). But how can businesses realize the data-driven culture on the ground? One technique to build the data-driven culture is to use the data to do the talking, and this can be done by building quality data sets. In this regard, below are the three key steps for building a data-driven culture in the enterprise.

Profile the data and fix data quality issues

In chapter 4, we discussed data profiling in detail. Data profiling is the process of examining the existing data available and collecting statistics about that data. Given that business data is normally distributed, these statistics on the profile of the data should cover not only the database related parameters, but also metrics such as standard deviation (on data accuracy), standard error (on data precision), range (on variation in data), average (mean, median, and mode), and z-score (for outliers in the data set).

In addition, during profiling, there might be some data quality issues, specifically on the 12 data quality dimensions. Here are three key tactics to fix the data quality: especially in the "after-the-event" situation.

1. Identify the data quality dimensions which are relevant as data quality is contextual. You don't have to fix all the issues on all the 12 data quality dimensions. For example, as discussed earlier, often accurate data is acceptable over correct data.

2. Fix data in the source system, that is, in the transactional system and not in the data warehouse. Often, data quality issues can be solved by cleaning up the original source. Data transfer and transpose (EAI and ETL) is a risk to data integrity and quality

3. To prevent the data quality issue from reoccurring, define data ownership at the point of data collection or creation. Quality data is highly correlated with creating data correctly the first time.

Once the data quality is improved, ensure that the right stakeholders have access to the right data. This can be done by classifying data according to the compliance view, which is of three main categories: public, confidential, and restricted data. If the data is sensitive, it must be protected, if not the access to the data can be opened.

Open the access to non-sensitive data

Once the enterprise data is profiled based on the compliance view, provide access to non-sensitive data to everyone in the company. When more data is available at the user's disposal, the chances of building a data-driven culture and data literacy is enhanced. The public data in the business is usually non-sensitive data. In addition, reference data and master data are typically non-sensitive data when compared to transactional data, which is usually sensitive due to its contextual nature. For example, while the dollar value in the purchase order, which is transactional data is sensitive, the vendor and item data in the purchase order, which is master data is not very sensitive. The table below is the categorization of non-sensitive data and sensitive data.

	Reference Data	Master Data	Transactional Data
Public Data	Non-sensitive data	Non-sensitive data	Non-sensitive data
Confidential Data	Non-sensitive data	Non-sensitive data	Sensitive data
Restricted Data	Sensitive data	Sensitive data	Sensitive data

Figure 7.3: Data sensitivity classification

Empower users to use data

One key strategy to empower business users is to leverage Self-Service Analytics (SSA). In SSA, business users perform queries and generate reports and dashboards on their own without relying much on the IT developers. SSA promises data democratization and faster data-based decisions. SSA does not eliminate IT-Business collaboration as some amount of training, governance, and change management is still required for the business from IT. The two main issues with SSA are data security and licensing of analytics tools.

Building data pipelines

A data pipeline is an extract of discrete and/or time-series data from multiple data sources and loading the data into the data warehouse or data lake for analytics. The data extract is with SQL stored procedures, which enables the data pipelines to quickly and efficiently extract data from the transactional source systems, transform it, and ingest it into data-warehouse or data-lake for deriving insights thereby improving the data literacy. Fundamentally, data pipelines bring reliability in the data integration process, thereby improving the trust in the way the data is sourced, transformed, and ingested.

The data pipeline architecture has three layers where each layer feeds into the next until data reaches its destination, which can be the data warehouse, data lake, or data hubs.

- **Extraction.** Data is extracted from transactional IT systems where the data is originated and captured.

- **Transformation.** Once data is extracted from source IT systems, its structure or format needs to be adjusted. Transformations include conversion, cleaning, populating, filtering, and aggregation of the extracted data.

- **Ingestion.** The ingestion layer reads data from each data source using application programming interfaces (APIs), and the data is ingested, either in batches or through streams into the data warehouse or data lake or data hubs.

Implementing reports and dashboards

Once the data is made available, the third capability in improving the data literacy in business is building reports and dashboards – the two pillars of descriptive analytics. Fundamentally, a report is a list of data attributes generated based on the criteria defined. Reports can be tabular reports where the data typically comes from the transactional IT systems like ERP or CRM system, or the reports can be from the BI systems where the data comes from a data warehouse or data lake. Fundamentally, tabular reports are presented as views in the data visualization layer; a view is the result set of a SQL query on the data. Tabular reports have four key characteristics.

- **Granular.** Tabular reports are granular, providing specific details of rows and even attributes as they are typically designed for the Analysts in the company. As the granular data is the lowest level of data, it can be molded in any way that the analyst requires. Apart from this, granular data can be easily merged with data from external sources and can be effectively integrated and managed.

- **Static.** Tabular reports have the data typically sourced from the transactional databases, and they display only certain fields of data within a specific domain.

- **Canned.** Tabular reports are usually canned reports which are pre-formatted and distributed to the whole organization or to specifically defined user groups. Canned reports allow the organization to generate scalable, print-ready reports for its users.

- **Analyst Centric.** Tabular reports are designed for analyst levels of users like an Accounts Payable (AP) Clerk or a Truck Dispatcher or a Trading Analyst to study or examine their respective functional areas in detail.

The second type of report is the BI report. BI reports provide features to sort, filter, group or aggregate, and visualize data across multiple dimensions. The data warehouses are denormalized databases in BI systems where the data extraction query does not have to go to multiple tables to get the right data. This saves a lot of querying time, thereby improving the speed of data rendering. BI reports are presented as cubes; a cube is stored data in a multi-dimensional form. Just like tabular reports which are on historical data, BI reports have four key characteristics.

- **Aggregation.** BI reports use aggregated data, that is, pre-calculated summary data, for key attributes or fields. Apart from data aggregation, BI reports also focus on the association between different variables.

- **Multi-dimensionality.** In the BI systems, data is stored in multiple dimensions or attributes as cubes enabling the user to look at the data holistically from many different perspectives. For example, with BI reports, the sales order data sets can be analyzed using different dimensions like region, year, amount, sales manager, and so on.

- **Ad-hoc Reporting.** With ad-hoc reporting, dynamic reports are generated by the user as and when needed. While the transactional reports have limited abilities to change the report, ad-hoc reports give users greater flexibility in querying the underlying data and how it should be presented.

- **Manager Centric.** BI reports usually cater to the manager level users as managers are entrusted with a leadership role with the responsibility of overseeing a department or group of employees within a specific department in the company. Managers need to analyze data quickly across various business dimensions, and BI reports give that capability.

So, when does one go for tabular reports, and when does one for go BI reports? If the requirements are for detailed or granular data, then the reports must be transactional, where the data is coming from the transactional systems. The need for transactional reports will usually come from the analysts. On the other hand, if the business users need aggregated and multi-dimensional data in a fast way or ad-hoc way, then BI reports are a good place to go! This need will usually come from middle and senior management. The image on the facing page shows the comparison between Transactional and BI reports.

While the reports (transactional and BI) are the presentation of the data on the database attributes, some users, especially the managers and the senior managers, require specific information to be presented quickly and visually as a KPI. To address the insight needs of these types of "monitor" users, the best practices are to go for dashboards. A dashboard fundamentally presents insights or KPIs in a visual manner. A typical dashboard will have four key types of insights, comparisons, trends, distribution, and relationships, and is visually presented using charts. The relationship between the four key types of dashboard insights and the 13 key visuals or charts is as shown below. The figure below is adapted from the work of Abela, A [Abela, 2009].

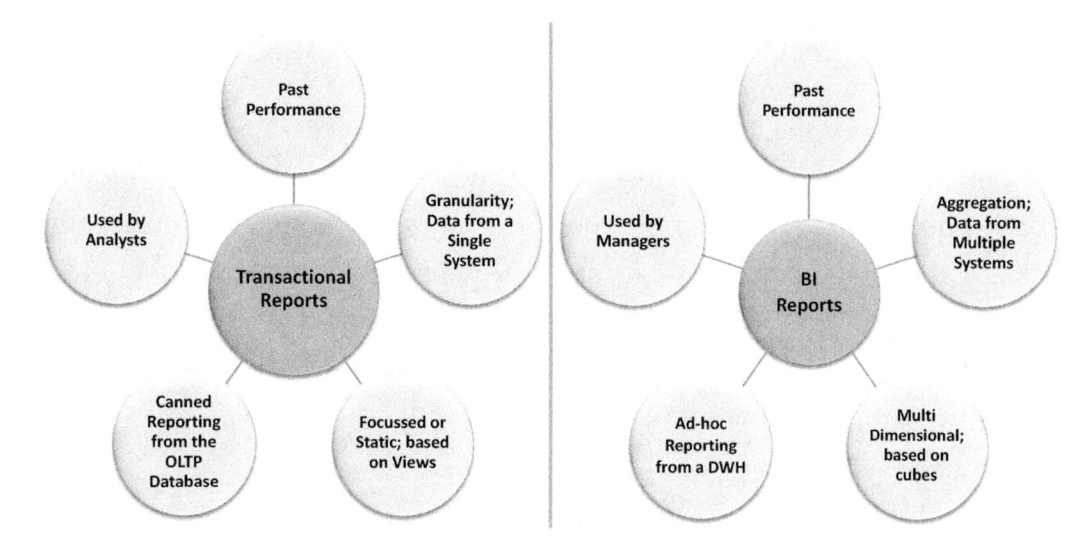

Figure 7.4: Transactional reports V/s BI reports

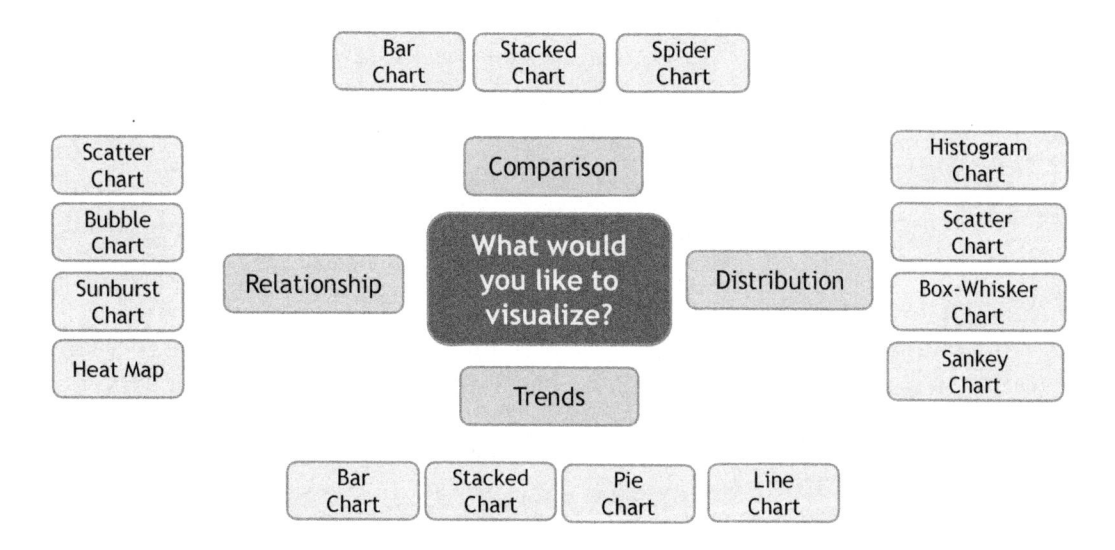

Figure 7.5: Visuals in dashboard

Conclusion

In the same way literacy has contributed to human progress, data literacy is essential in ensuring the progress or the growth of the organization in today's data-centric world. What is even more important is that today understanding data and deriving insights in business operations is no longer the skill of just data scientists and IT experts. It is an essential or core skill for every knowledge worker if the company wants to leverage data for improved business performance and become data-driven.

References

- Abela, A, "Chart Suggestions—A Thought-Starter," https://bit.ly/33Znj3t.
- Bean, Randy and Davenport, Thomas, "Companies Are Failing in Their Efforts to Become Data-Driven," Harvard Business Review, Feb 2019.
- Ericsson, Anders; Prietula, Michael; Cokely, Edward, "Making of an Expert," Harvard Business Review, Jul 2007.
- Gartner, "A Data and Analytics Leader's Guide to Data Literacy ", https://gtnr.it/39yRShA, Feb 2019.
- IBM, "Descriptive, predictive, prescriptive: Transforming asset and facilities management with analytics," https://ibm.co/2JwQzFi, 2017.
- Jain, Piyanka and Sharma, Puneet "Behind Every Good Decision: How Anyone Can Use Business Analytics to Turn Data into Profitable Insights," AMACOM, 2014.
- Williamson, Jason, "Getting a Big Data Job For Dummies," Wiley, 2015.

CHAPTER 8

Best Practice #7

Use Continuous Refinement and Validation as the Mainstay of Advanced Analytics

"Prediction is very difficult, especially if it's about the future."

Niels Bohr

Predictive and prescriptive analytics together form advanced analytics. Predictive analytics is making predictions about the future based on historical data to identify risks and opportunities. Given that planning is one of the key functions of management on the future direction of the company, predictive analytics enables business enterprises to proactively anticipate business outcomes, behaviors, and events to better plan, influence, and respond. While predictive analytics is predicting the future event, prescriptive analytics is finding the best course of action for a given situation using optimization techniques to address constraints and trade-offs. Predictive and prescriptive analytics are used in almost every industry. Examples include asset failure (Oil & Gas), fraud detection (Banking), customer churn (Retail), predicting epidemics (HealthCare), prediction of weather patterns (Agriculture), to name few.

Let us first discuss the first element of advanced analytics - predictive analytics. Technically, predictive analytics is predicting one targeted or dependent variable based on several independent predictors or variables. Predictive analytics can broadly be grouped into two areas:

1. Analyst-driven or Regression techniques
2. Data-driven or Machine Learning (ML) techniques.

With analyst driven or regression techniques, the focus is on establishing an analytics model to represent the relationships between the independent and the dependent variables. Depending on the question and the data type, there are a wide variety of regression models such as linear regression, logistic regression, polynomial regression, and so on that can be applied while performing predictive analytics.

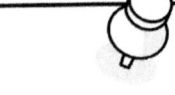

> ML is moving to data-driven analytics.
>
> This means ML is dependent on your organization's automation capabilities.

Machine learning (ML), employs techniques to enable computers to learn from data without being explicitly programmed. ML works out the predictions and recalibrates models in near real-time automatically, while the analyst-driven predictive analytics models work strictly on "cause" data and must be refreshed with "changed" data. There are two main types of ML techniques: Supervised ML and Unsupervised ML.

- In Supervised ML, the data scientist guides the algorithm on the outputs the algorithm should come up with. Supervised ML requires that the algorithm's possible outputs are already known and that the data used to train the algorithm is already labeled with the correct answers. For example, in the retail industry context, a classification algorithm, which is a type of Supervised ML, will be used to identify products after being trained on a dataset of images that are properly labeled with the product type and some identifying characteristics.

- Unsupervised ML is more closely aligned with true artificial intelligence (AI) — the idea that a computer can learn to identify complex processes and patterns without a data scientist to provide guidance along the way. For example, unsupervised ML can be used for customer segmentation because it will return groups based on parameters that a data scientist may not consider due to his/her pre-existing biases on the past sales performance, economic factors, competition, and other factors.

The second element of advanced analytics is prescriptive analytics. Prescriptive analysis works on the independent variables to achieve the best possible outcome and then prescribes the best course of action using optimization techniques. Optimization techniques enable minimizing or maximizing the objectives or performance criteria. There are two different types of optimization methods:

1. Exact optimization methods
2. Heuristic optimization methods.

Exact optimization methods determine an optimal solution by maximizing or minimizing the performance criteria. Exact optimization techniques include the Simplex and Gauss-Newton methods. In Heuristic optimization methods, there is no guarantee that an optimal solution will be found. It gives sub-optimal solutions. Common heuristic optimization techniques are Genetic algorithms and Ant-colony algorithms.

Predictive and prescriptive analytics are co-dependent disciplines; they are NOT mutually exclusive. IBM says - predictive and prescriptive analytics go together like birds of a feather [Kuttappa, 2019]. Predictive analytics helps in identifying the variables that impact the future, while prescriptive analytics provides options where one can weigh the variables against one another. Predictive analytics forecasts what might happen in the future with an acceptable level of reliability, while prescriptive analytics will help in identifying the optimal set of variables. In business management, these variables are often business resources like time, money, and labor.

For example, in multiple linear regression (MLR), the model reliability and the independent variable selection is based on threshold levels set for metrics like r-square, P-value, F-value, standard error, and standard deviation. The variables selected using the above criteria to form the MLR regression model meet the statistical criteria, but they are not the optimal list of variables that can maximize or minimize the outcome. The optimal set of independent variables can be selected with what-if scenarios in prescriptive analytics such that the business resources are optimized.

Let us take an example of applying predictive and prescriptive analytics in the trucking or the freight industry. Predictive analytics can be used to make availability forecasts of when the shipping containers would become available for pickup at terminals. But the next step is dispatching and scheduling the fleet of truckers for the actual pickup, and this is where prescriptive analytics come into the picture. Another example where the predictive and prescriptive analytics are often used together is in the oil industry. Oil refineries apply predictive analytics techniques to predict the price of crude oil and refined oil products like gasoline and diesel. Based on the predicted prices, refineries apply prescriptive analytics techniques to determine the best way to blend the crude oil feed to maximize revenue under constraints like environmental regulations, contractual demands of the gas stations, and so on.

Why is this a best practice?

As predictive and prescriptive analytics is about predicting the future and optimizing the variables; the insights or output always have a degree of likelihood or probabilities and not absolute certainties. Hence the insights in both predictive and prescriptive analytics have some degree of uncertainty, that is, measurement of variability in the data. This uncertainty usually comes from two key sources: Systematic error and Random error

The systematic error occurs because of the imperfections in the data analytics value chain such as goal formulation, data collection, data integration, statistical analysis, to name a few. Random error, on the other hand, occurs because of the unknown, uncontrollable, and unpredictable reasons. While the systematic error can be reduced and controlled, random error is often difficult to reduce or eliminate as it is unpredictable.

But businesses despise uncertainty, especially the uncertainty that is associated with the systematic error. Given that both predictive and prescriptive analytics are inherently probabilistic, businesses look for capabilities or practices where the uncertainty in the process can be reduced or even eliminated. A best practice to deal with uncertainty is to go for the continuous refinement and validation of the output values coming out from predictive and prescriptive analytics.

Realizing the best practice

As the real or the actual values in both predictive and prescriptive analytics will be available only in the future, we need options to often validate the solution. So what strategies are available for continuously refining and validating the advanced analytics models? There are three main strategies here:

1. Cross-validation of data
2. Validation of output from multiple algorithms
3. What-if scenarios on the variables.

Cross-validation of data

Cross-validation is a statistical technique of splitting or partitioning or folding the data into subsets – training and test. The training data is used to train and build the prediction model, while the test data is used to evaluate the performance of the prediction model. To reduce variability in the output, multiple rounds of cross-validation are performed with different combinations of data subsets. The fundamental idea of cross-validation is to hide one part of the data, learn on the rest, and then check or validate the "knowledge" on what was hidden.

Let us look at the above process in more detail. As mentioned above, the available dataset is randomly partitioned into two sets: training data sets and test data sets. The training data set is the larger data set, which is about 80% of the data, and the testing data set is a smaller data set, which is the remaining 20% of the data. The training data is again randomly divided into "N" smaller blocks. Each time "N-1" training subsets are chosen, and the one remaining data subset becomes the test data subset. The output derived using (N-1) training subset data is validated against the test subset data. On the next run, the former test subset becomes one of the training subsets for deriving the output, and one of the former training subsets becomes the test data subset to validate the output. The process continues until all the data subsets are utilized either as training or test subsets to have a robust "trained" analytics model.

Once there is a "trained" analytics model, we come back to the initial state where the data was divided into 80% training dataset and 20% test data set. The data in the testing data set already contains known values for the Y (dependent or the target variable). The analytics model is executed and validated against the 20% test data to determine whether the model's prediction or output is valid. The cross-validation process is as shown in Figure 8.1.

Output validation from multiple algorithms

While cross-validation deals with input, that is, the data to feed the analytics model, the second-best practice deals with algorithms. To have a robust analytics model, one must confirm the output from multiple algorithms or statistical models. For example, even though simple and multiple linear regression algorithms are the most popular prediction analytics algorithms, there are other prediction algorithms like Logistic Regression, ARIMA (AutoRegressive Integrated Moving Average), CART (Classification and Regression Trees), SVM (Support vector machines), and so on. As discussed in the first chapter, analytics is using data to answer business questions to get insights. Getting insights is dependent on the algorithms selected, and the selection of the algorithm is largely dependent on the question formulated and the data type.

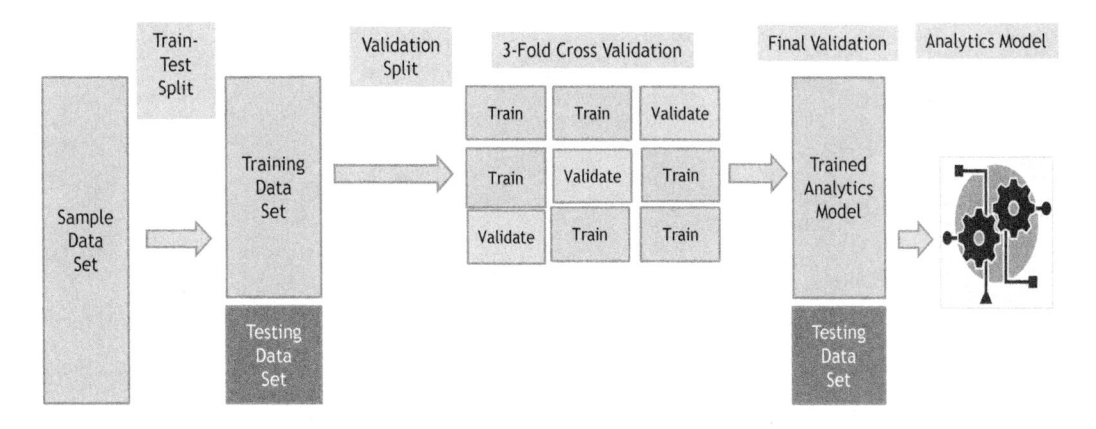

Figure 8.1: Data splitting and cross-validation

How the question is formulated, and the type of data, determines the algorithm selected? Say the business question is – will my retail store in Denver, Colorado, make a profit in January of 2022? As the business question is a binary classification question, profit or loss, logistic regression is the recommended algorithm. However, along with logistic regression, SVM (Support vector machine) algorithm can also be used to get insights and classify the store as a profitable one or not. In this way, we can have multiple algorithms confirming the same result. Here is an example, where SAS Viya, a leading analytics software used multiple algorithms and suggested that gradient boosting, a type of regression and classification algorithm is the recommended algorithm for a particular use case of customer churn in a retail chain.

"Model Comparison" Results

mpion	Name	Algorithm Name	KS (Youden)
⊠	Gradient Boosting	Gradient Boosting	0.8587
	Decision Tree	Decision Tree	0.6900
	Forward Logistic Regression	Logistic Regression	0.5636
	Stepwise Logistic Regression	Logistic Regression	0.5636

Figure 8.2: Output validation from multiple algorithms in SAS Viya

What-if scenarios

The third strategy of realizing this best practice is in applying the what-if scenarios. Predictive analytics predicts the output of the dependent variable using independent variables. As mentioned before, in businesses, these independent variables are often resources like money, time, energy, products, materials, and land. Given that business management is about optimal resource management, these variables or resources selected must be optimized. Basically, there are two steps here: variable selection and variable optimization.

On the variable selection step, multi-collinearity and overfitting techniques ensure that the independent variables selected in the prediction model are valid and can be considered for optimization. Multicollinearity is a state of very high inter-associations among the independent variables resulting in one or more independent variables being redundant. Overfitting is a phenomenon when the analytics model has "learned" too much from the training data and does not perform well in practice as a result. Overfitting is usually caused by the model having too much exposure to the training data. The second step is to get an optimized variable set. Once we have the list of independent variables selected, different 'what if' scenarios can help in identifying the best or optimized future scenarios. 'What-if' scenarios, also known as sensitivity analysis, is basically asking questions on the most likely future situations businesses need to manage. Technically, 'What- if' scenarios analyze how the different values of independent variables affect the dependent variable or output under certain specific conditions or constraints. The sensitivity analysis estimates how sensitive the dependent variable is to a change in an independent variable(s). As the independent variables are resources and resources are typically constrained in business, what-if analysis provides insights on how the resources can be optimally managed.

Below is an example of the application of what-if analysis in the calculation of the firm valuation, that is, terminal valuation (TV). The TV is calculated using two input variables, IGR (industry growth rate) and WACC (weighted average cost of capital). For example, if the IGR is 4% and if the WACC is 13%, then the TV of the firm is US$ 2888.89 million. On the other hand, if the IGR is 1% and if the WACC is 15%, then the TV of the firm will be US$ 1803.57 million.

2861.111	0.08	0.09	0.1	0.11	0.12	0.13	0.14	0.15
0	3125	2777.778	2500	2272.727	2083.333	1923.077	1785.714	1666.667
0.01	3607.143	3156.25	2805.556	2525	2295.455	2104.167	1942.308	1803.571
0.02	4250	3642.857	3187.5	2833.333	2550	2318.182	2125	1961.538
0.03	5150	4291.667	3678.571	3218.75	2861.111	2575	2340.909	2145.833
0.04	6500	5200	4333.333	3714.286	3250	2888.889	2600	2363.636
0.05	8750	6562.5	5250	4375	3750	3281.25	2916.667	2625

(rows: IGR; columns: WACC)

Figure 8.3: Sensitivity analysis

Conclusion

Advanced analytics, which is a combination of predictive analytics and prescriptive analytics, is inherently probabilistic in nature. This means there is subjectivity and uncertainty in the output, or the insights derived. This uncertainty can be minimized by continuously validating and refining the analytics model. In addition, there is an increasing emphasis on monetizing data these days by optimizing business resource consumption. While there are many approaches, one of the ways to monetize data is to leverage advanced analytics, that is, predictive and prescriptive analytics techniques, and use the business resources optimally. The next chapter will cover more on data monetization. But the fundamentals of the advanced analytics remain the same as basic or descriptive analytics; the data quality needs to be good, and the outputs must be constantly refined and validated before the insights can be consumed in the most optimal manner.

References

- Bean, Randy and Davenport, Thomas, "Companies Are Failing in Their Efforts to Become Data-Driven," Harvard Business Review, Feb 2019.
- Uthappa, Sajan "Why prescriptive analytics and decision optimization are crucial," https://ibm.co/2wQvrY5, Apr 2019.

CHAPTER 9

Best Practice #8

Leverage Analytics for Data Monetization

> *"California's consumers should have a share in the wealth that is created from their data."*
>
> *California Governor Gavin Newsom*

Today most companies have access to large volumes of data related to their operations, compliance activities, business entities like suppliers, customers, and competitors, and much more. The enormous amount of data that is collected on business operations offers possibilities for monetization. Data monetization is the process of leveraging data to generate monetary value from raw data or data-based solutions. According to Gartner, data monetization is using data for quantifiable economic benefit. This can include indirect methods such as improving business performance, leveraging beneficial terms or conditions from business partners, information bartering, productizing information, "informationalizing" products, or selling data outright [Gartner, 2020].

Is data monetization a new concept? Although still nascent in some industries, data monetization is already prevalent in many industry sectors, especially those sectors that are in the B2C (Business to Consumer) segment. Today, companies such as Facebook, Amazon, and Google derive a significant portion of their revenue from the user data they have captured. These companies harvest massive amounts of data about their users and then provide this data for a fee to the advertisers. This is a classic or traditional case of data monetization from consumers. Is this ethical and legal? It might not be ethical for some people, but as of today, it is legal. However, California's Governor Gavin Newsom proposes "a new data dividend" that could allow California's consumers to get paid for their digital data from companies such as Facebook and Google. The data dividend proposal follows the California state legislature's passage of the data privacy bill, granting consumers specific rights related to their personal data [CNBC, 2019]. It is not just the consumer or user data that can be monetized. For example, today monetizing car data is a common data monetization topic as cars generate various types of data such as how they are used, where they are and who is behind the wheel. As a result, several players associated in the automotive industry try to turn car data to create data related products and services. Mckinsey finds that the global revenue pool from car data monetization could be as high as US$ 750 billion by 2030 [Mckinsey, 2016].

SPS Commerce, a retail analytics firm, provides cloud-based supply chain management software in a digital network that includes more than 90,000 retail, distribution, grocery, and e-commerce companies. SPS collects retail PoS data from retail chains like Walmart, Loblaw, Amazon, and Costco. SPS then monetizes this data by converting the data into insight reports on product sales and supply chain operations and selling the insight reports to CPG companies like P&G, Nestle, Pepsi, Kraft Foods, and Coca-Cola.

Why is this a best practice?

As discussed earlier, the three key purposes of data in business are to support the business in operations, compliance, and decision making. Why should a business enterprise monetize its data? What are the drivers to use data other than its core purpose which is using data for insights, compliance, and operations? At the highest or strategy level, data monetization in business helps in increasing revenue, reducing cost, and mitigating risk. But at the tactical level, there are three main reasons for pursuing data monetization in business.

Firstly, data monetization refocuses the business enterprise to accomplish its primary goal - maximizing returns for the investors. Even in today's world of CSR (Corporate Social Responsibility) and TBL (Triple Bottom Line), maximizing profit remains one of the core objectives of running a business. Data management fundamentally is a tactical endeavor, and data monetization can link the strategic goal of maximizing profit for the shareholders to the tactics. Given that data is a business asset, companies should look at every possibility of harnessing this intangible business asset for better financial results. Secondly, data monetization helps to optimize asset performance as efficient asset utilization is one of the core functions of the business. Even though we see a new data-centric economy, data is still an under-utilized business asset in most companies. Historically, companies have managed tangible assets such as land, plants, equipment, and inventory. In today's digital world, data is a new asset that companies must manage well. However, most companies are leaving money on the table, with only one in 12 companies monetizing data to its fullest extent [Gandhi et al., 2018]. Thirdly, focusing on data monetization improves business efficiency. Managing data is an expensive process. Unfortunately, many companies are collecting data without a clear objective. Forrester says 73% of the data collected in business is never used for any strategic purposes [Gualtieri, 2016]. If the data collected by the business is not monetizable, data can even become a liability, as seen in the cases of Equifax, CapitalOne, and Target. So basically, focusing on data monetization will position the business to become efficient, thereby reducing its SG&A (Selling, General, and Administrative) expenses and minimizing the risk in business operations.

Realizing the best practice

Today monetizing data effectively— can be a source of competitive advantage in the digital economy. While companies such as Facebook, Amazon, and Google leverage user data for a fee from advertisers, all enterprises cannot turn their data into a monetizable asset in this manner. According to data monetization expert, Doug Laney, "Managing information as an asset involves applying traditional asset management principles and practices to information. This can involve adapting physical, financial, human capital, or other asset management methods. And measuring information as an asset is about gauging an information asset's quality characteristics, business relevance, impact on KPIs, along with applying traditional accounting valuation methods." [Laney, 2017].

Fundamentally data monetization is solving a business problem using data for improved business performance. The monetary value could come from creating new revenue streams, or it could be in the reduction in the cost of operations, savings in the time spent in running the business, or in mitigating risk in business operations. In this regard, there are three primary paths to data monetization in business enterprises:

1. Data architecture
2. Embedded analytics
3. Data products

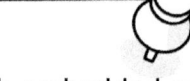

> Both embedded analytics and data products rely on user personas.
>
> User personas offer a realistic representation of the needs, experiences, and behaviors of the stakeholders.

Data architecture

In today's digital economy, business enterprises strive to maximize the value of data for improved business performance. Data architecture is a key enabler for an enterprise to become data-driven. It is the practice of designing, building, and optimizing data-driven systems by incorporating the company's vision, strategies, business rules, standards, and capabilities to manage the data. While many progressive and proactive organizations have the data architecture capability within the CDO (Chief Data Officer) function, there are still some organizations that are yet to take that plunge. This section looks at the importance and needs for a good data architecture in a business enterprise for effective data monetization.

Why should the business care for a data architecture? How is data architecture tied to data monetization? Data architecture looks at data monetization for improved business efficiency by offering solid strategies for companies to effectively manage their data across the entire DLC. Specifically, data architecture offers three key benefits to the business.

- **Enabling data strategy**. Strategy, in general, is considering alternatives and making trade-offs to pick the best option. A strong data strategy needs to be underpinned by a flexible and scalable data architecture that aligns with company strategies, compliance requirements, business rules, technology, capability, skills, and internal enterprise architecture standards. A key element in the data strategy is the current data landscape in the company, and data architecture offers that landscape as an enterprise data model (EDM). An effective EDM is based on the integrated business value chain with key data objects (reference, master, and transactional data) represented in each of the value chain elements. In addition, data architecture helps in deciding the right data strategy to move to the future state by considering the company's strategies, business rules, technologies, standards, and capabilities.

> Data Quality at an enterprise level is always assessed against the enterprise data model (EDM).
>
> Hence do not start any data quality assessment without the EDM.

- **Improved communication and collaboration.** As discussed in chapter 2, as part of best practice #1, a typical business enterprise has various stakeholders having different roles, needs, priorities, and constraints. This often results in various lines of business and even creates data silos in the company, which is further exuberated by mergers and acquisitions (M&A). Also, for the most part, business enterprises operate within various assumptions and constraints. So, when stakeholders from various functions, geographies, and competing needs come together, businesses need a data architecture that can be a glue that provides a common language for improved communication and collaboration.

- **Creating optimal information flows.** As data architecture provides a holistic view of the data flows in the enterprise – current and future, it provides opportunities for creating lean and optimal information flows by eliminating complexity, reusing data, and minimizing data/system redundancy. This ultimately results in reduced cost, minimized risk, and faster time to market for the products and services.

They say, "start with the end in mind"; one cannot build a sky-scrapper without an architecture. In today's data-centric business world, the digital journey for the business starts with a solid data architecture - the foundation for data monetization for a sustainable competitive advantage. So, what is contained in the Data Architecture? According to TOGAF (The Open Group Architecture Framework), the Data Architecture should at least comprise of two key elements [TOGAF, 2020]:

- The Enterprise Data Model (EDM) – the combination of business and logical data models

- Data management process model and data entity-business function matrix. This is the Value Stream Mapping (VSM) concept which was discussed earlier in chapter 6.

Embedded analytics

The second data monetization capability is on realizing Embedded Analytics (EA). EA primarily looks at data monetization based on the time saved in consuming the insights in business operations. In most business enterprises, BI applications and transactional applications are entirely separate systems. This forces users to switch between the two IT systems; the user accesses the BI system to get insights and then uses the transactional system(s) to act. Multiple applications are used to derive insights and act. This results in a significant amount of time consumed to access insights and act. Nucleus Research estimates that switching from the transactional system to the BI system to get business insights wastes up to two hours per employee each week [Moxie, 2016].

> The term real-time insight is a misnomer.
>
> There is always some amount of time lag or delay in insight derivation.

It is not just the employee time wasted; it is also the lost business opportunity due to the cost of delay (CoD). CoD is a metric that measures the impact of time on the outcomes. In short, CoD is the leakage in value over time. CoD is closely tied to the opportunity costs, which is the loss of potential gain from other alternatives when one alternative is chosen.

This is where embedded analytics comes into play. EA, which is the integration of insights within the transactional applications, so users can work closely with the insights in the transactional applications they use every day. Technically, EA is the insertion into the UI (User Interface) of the OLTP (Online Transactional Processing) system or the SoR (System of Record) the insights from the SoI (System of Insight) systems. Apart from the UI design, embedded analytics relies on API (Application Programming Interface) and Identity Management (IDM) functionalities for seamless consumption of insights in the transactional or SoR systems. API is a software intermediary that allows two systems to talk to each other. IDM describes the management of individual identities, their authentication, authorization, roles, and privileges.

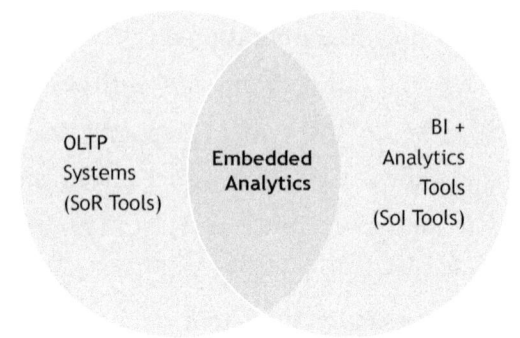

Figure 9.1: Embedded analytics

Below is a simple example of EA, which is geo-triggered or location-based push notifications which are triggered when a user physically moves near a Sephora store –a personal care and beauty store [MacFarlane, 2019]. These notifications, which are often done through either geofencing or beacons, offer personalized, timely, and location-based push campaigns based on the insight that the user is physically close to the store.

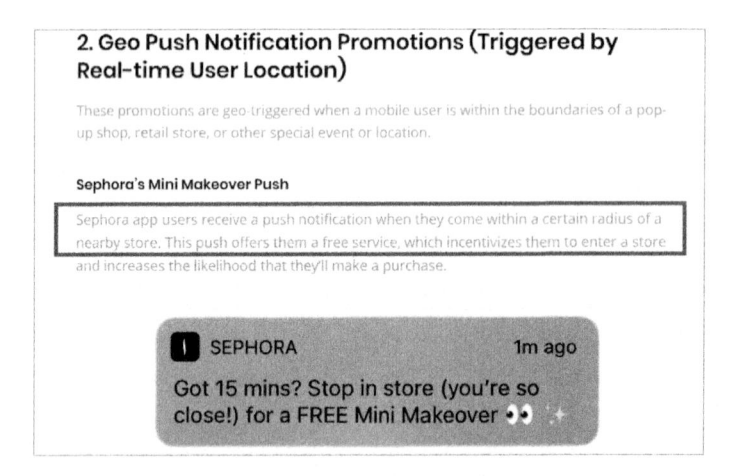

Figure 9.2: Application of embedded insights

Data products

The third data monetization capability is to develop data products. A data product is the application of data for improving business performance; it is usually an output of the data science activity. There are three types of data products.

- **Data enhancing products**. These data products capture and catalog data from a variety of sources. As these data sets grow, they become very valuable. Also known as data brokers or data hubs, the data enhancing products aggregate data from a variety of sources, cleanse it, and process it for consumption. Ex: IHS Markit, Expedia, and IEA (International Energy Agency) offer data enhancing products

- **Data exchanging products**. Here, users create data in exchange for a more valuable set of data back. The more data one shares with these products or platforms, the better is the value these products offer to the users. Ex: Facebook, LinkedIn, eBay, Amazon, etc.

- **Data experiencing products**. These data products use a combination of data, integration APIs, proprietary algorithms, and analytics for better insights and business outcomes. The data experiencing platforms can be of two types.
    - External products. For example, Bloomberg gives accurate and market-based commodity prices.
    - Internal products like Sales-Margin Reports, Spend- Reports, and so on.

Building a data experiencing data product is relatively easy compared to building data enhancing or data exchanging product as the control and influence is usually inside the organization, and the impact can be seen quickly. While data experiencing data product will not create new revenue streams for the company, it will potentially improve efficiencies, expose value leaks, and reduce operational risks for the company.

According to Gartner, during the fourth version of the CDO, CDO 4.0, businesses should focus on data products, and on managing profit and loss using data products instead of just being responsible for driving data analytics projects and programs. Data products scale data and analytics capabilities, hiding the complexity in data management and other organizational constraints and offer the opportunity to deliver transformational value to the enterprise.

Building data products are based on two key elements: strong value proposition and high-quality data. The strong value proposition comes from looking at the entire value chain holistically and identifying value leakages. Value leakages typically happen when there is a hand-over or transition from one value stream in the VSM, and the transition often results in the misalignment of processes, peoples' skills, KPIs, and data. VSM was discussed in chapter 6.

The second element in building data products is associated with high-quality data. As discussed before, high-quality data means the data that is used in the data product is subject to the 12 key data quality dimensions discussed in best practice #4. The high-level steps in building a data experiencing internal product for a business enterprise is shown in Figure 9.3.

Typically, when building data products, there will be compliance issues involved in data monetization such as privacy and security. The compliance issues pertaining to the data can be addressed using data manipulating techniques such as encryption, anonymization, scrambling, tokenizing, and masking which will potentially remove the sensitivities in the data.

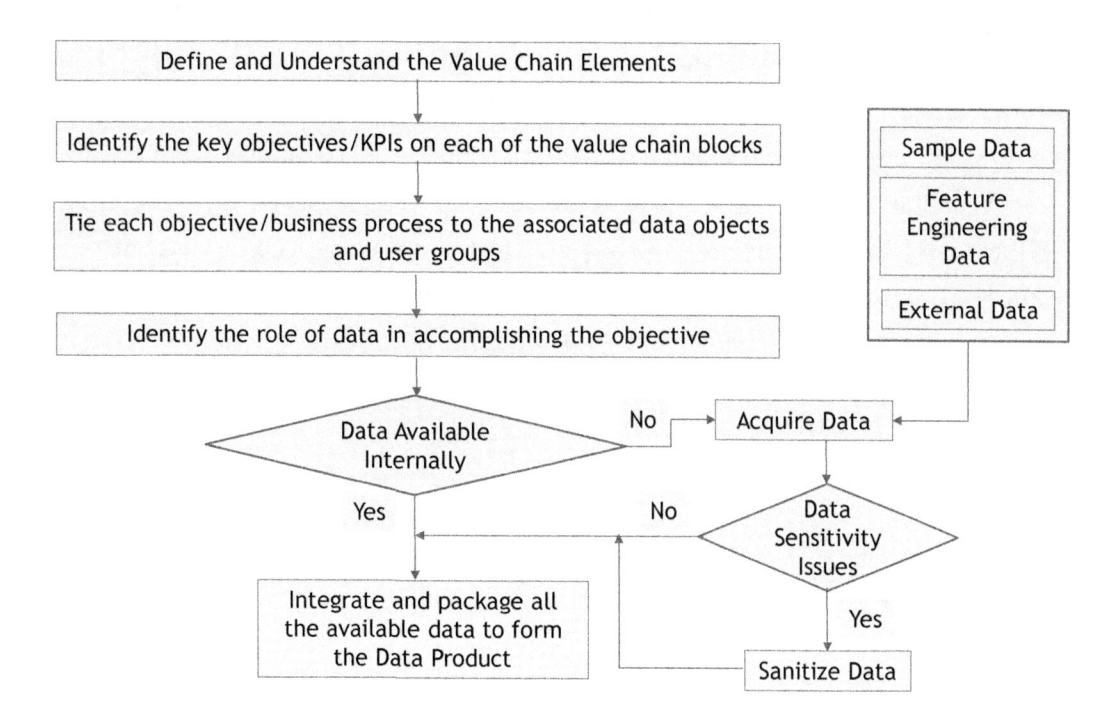

Figure 9.3: Building data experiencing products

Conclusion

Today, almost all companies want to leverage data for building sustainable competitive advantage. Data will not give a company that competitive advantage. The company needs to position the data for competitive advantage. But how? Companies must treat data as a valuable business resource by focussing on three key elements – value, rarity, and non-substitutable, which was discussed in chapter 1. If these three core elements are not built in the data strategy, the data will not offer that competitive advantage and the capability to monetize data.

Fundamentally data monetization is not just making money from data; it is a new way of thinking for enhanced business productivity. It is about creating a sustainable competitive advantage for the business. However, data monetization is at an early stage of adoption in most companies. Enterprises are beginning to see that the benefits of data monetization are many—from creating new revenue streams, development of new services, quicker time-to-market, reducing the cost of business operations, and minimizing risk. However poor data quality and data compliance issues represent the two biggest obstacles to monetizing data. Companies that find ways to address these two challenges, will be able to better monetize their data and provide more value to their stakeholders.

References

- CNBC, "California governor proposes 'new data dividend' that could call on Facebook and Google to pay users," https://cnb.cx/2Uxm4Wr, Feb 2019.
- Gartner, "Fuel Digital Business with Product Management," https://gtnr.it/2JrGcml, Mar 2015.
- Gartner Glossary, https://gtnr.it/2UA9TrX, 2020.
- Gualtieri, Mike, "Hadoop Is Data's Darling for a Reason," https://bit.ly/2JrGkCl, Jan 2016.
- Laney, Douglas, "Infonomics: How to Monetize, Manage, and Measure Information as an Asset for Competitive Advantage," Routledge, Sep 2017.
- MacFarlane, Kate, "18 Inspiring Location-based Push Notifications," https://bit.ly/2wJmksi, Apr 2019.
- Mckinsey Report, "Monetizing car data," https://mck.co/39yS6oW, Sept 2016.
- Moxie, Anne, "Augmenting intelligence with Embedded Analytics," Nucleus Research, Dec 2016.
- Suketu Gandhi, Bharath Thota, Renata Kuchembuck, and Joshua Swartz. "Demystifying Data Monetization," Sloan Management Review, Nov 2018.
- TOGAF, "Information Systems Architectures - Data Architecture," https://pubs.opengroup.org/architecture/togaf91-doc/arch/chap10.html, 2020

CHAPTER 10

Best Practice #9

Support Analytics with Enterprise Data Governance

> *"For data only two moments really matter- the moment of data creation and the moment of data use. And they both don't happen in IT."*
>
> Tom Redman

Today, businesses create a large and varied amount of data. If the data that is ingested into the IT systems is not taken care of or governed, there will be a poor quality of data in the enterprise, ultimately resulting in poor business results. Data governance is a system of decision rights and accountabilities for information-related processes, executed according to agreed-upon models which describe who can take what actions with what information, and when, under what circumstances, using what methods [DGI, 2020]. At a tactical level, data governance is the collection of policies, processes, roles, standards, and KPIs that ensure high-quality data is used across the business organization in a compliant way.

In simple words, data governance is the right people managing the data in the right manner in accordance with the nine key data governance principles or areas listed below.

1. User identification is the management of the digital identities of users in the IT system(s)

2. User authentication is the process of verifying the user's identification
3. User authorization is the function of specifying access rights or privileges to users
4. Data confidentiality is protecting data against unauthorized access, disclosure, or theft
5. Data integrity is data that must be reliable and accurate over its entire lifecycle
6. Data availability is the ability to ensure that data is always accessible when needed in IT Systems
7. Nonrepudiation of data is logging of changes to the data values by the user(s) or the system(s)
8. Compliance to internal business rules – processes, rules, and controls
9. Compliance with external and industry standards.

Why is this a best practice?

> Data transfer and transpose (EAI & ETL) is a risk to the integrity of the data.
>
> Basically, data integrity is at risk when the data moves from one system to another.

Why is governing data a best analytics practice? There are three main reasons for companies to govern data. Firstly, today data is created in business at a rapid pace through different mechanisms and channels. This is resulting in a huge and a complex amount of data, causing data inconsistencies that need to be identified and addressed.

Secondly, data literacy and self-service analytics (SSA) are creating the need for a common definition and understanding of data across the organization. The democratization of data and analytics is creating an increasing need for a common and standard data model to enable better communication in the enterprise.

Thirdly, businesses need to adhere to compliance requirements like regulatory mandates (such as SOX, GDPR, and HIPAA), industry standards (such as ISO/IEC 38500 and UNSPSC), and even internal business policies. Without effective data governance, the data inconsistencies in different IT systems in the organization might not get resolved. For example, customer names may be listed differently in CRM, ERP, and customer service IT systems. This could complicate data integration efforts and create data integrity issues that affect the quality of the insights derived.

Data governance provides processes, roles, policies, standards, and KPIs that ensure high-quality data in the business. An enterprise data governance program typically results in the development of common data definitions and internal data standards that are applied in all business systems, boosting data consistency for both business and compliance uses. Also, data governance promotes strong compliance with security and privacy, which is achieved by locating critical data, identifying data owners and data users, and assessing and remediating risk to critical data assets.

> Data governance can be made effective with MDM which creates lean information flows.
>
> With MDM, if the data is right, you have one place to source data. If the data is wrong, you have one place to correct it!

Realizing the best practice

Effective data governance takes an efficient combination of people, process, and technology on how data is generated, stored, used, and maintained across the data lifecycle (DLC). There are three key capabilities in implementing data governance in the enterprise.

1. Identify the data assets to be governed
2. Identifying the data owner, stewards, and custodians of these data assets
3. Set up the process and KPIs to govern these data assets

Identify the data assets to be governed

As discussed in best practice #3, there are many types of data assets in a business enterprise – reference data on business categories, master data for business entities, and transactional data on the business events. The first step in data governance is to identify the specific categories of data objects to govern. While the specific data type to govern depends on the industry sector and the business need, data governance works effectively when the data assets are managed early in the data lifecycle. Specifically, data governance should identify the reference data (on business categories), and master data (on business entities) as these data elements are shared and used enterprise-wide in business transactions like purchase orders, sales orders, and invoices.

Data governance practices should first ensure high quality of reference data and master data in the enterprise. Data quality will be high when the data is initially created and captured. The moment data starts getting shared with different LoB and IT systems, then managing the data quality becomes challenging. A simplified example of a data flow diagram in a business enterprise is as shown in the figure below. The need for data governance is high

> Software is basically a window to the data.
>
> The software provides a consistent and secure way of capturing and managing data.

in the transactional or data capture systems, that is, in the initial stages of the DLC. The result is that data quality will also be high.

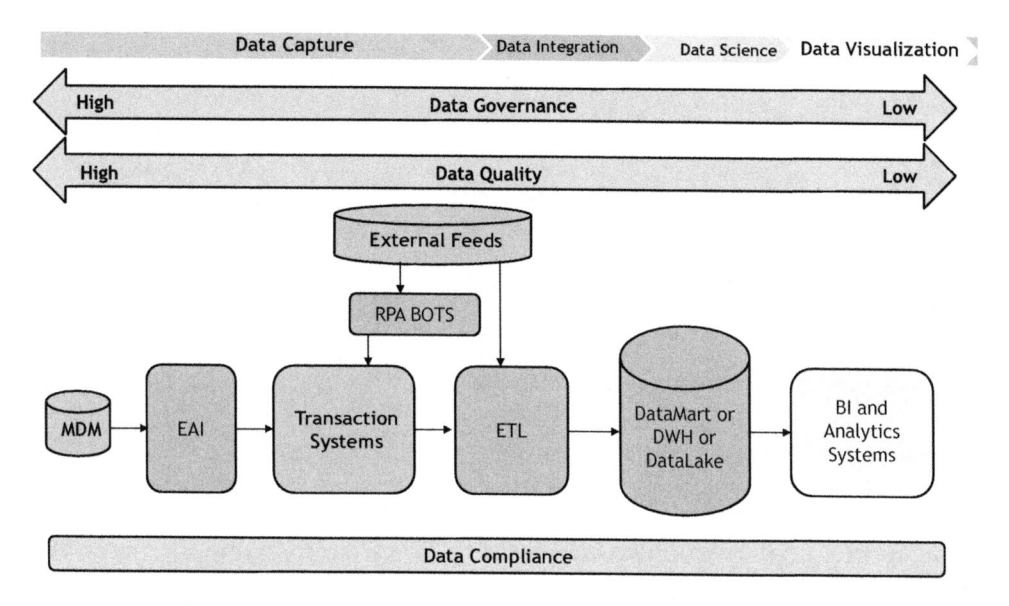

Figure 10.1: Simplified data flow

Identifying the data owner, stewards, and custodians of these data assets

Data governance must be led by the data owners and supported by data stewards from the business and data custodians from IT. All three, data owners, data stewards, and data custodians, should jointly take responsibility for the quality of the data in the enterprise. But what exactly is the role of the data owner, data steward, and data custodian?

- Data owners are ultimately accountable for the state of the data as an asset. They make decisions associated with the quality of the data asset.

- Data stewards are a business-driven role responsible for the content (nomenclatures), context (taxonomy), and associated business rules and attributes (ontology) to help set up quality data. The data steward who is responsible for the data quality, acts as a liaison between the IT department and the data or insight consumers by defining data formats, resolving data quality issues, and ensuring that data adheres to the defined internal and industry standards.

- Data custodians who are usually from the IT are responsible for the safe storage and transport of data. Primarily, data custodians are responsible for data security activities like authentication and authorization, data storage activities like data archiving, back-up, disaster recovery, and so on, and data transfer and transpose activities like EAI and ETL.

Data custodians work with data stewards to gain a better understanding of the business and data requirements. In short, data stewards are responsible for the content in the database, while data custodians are responsible for the technical environment of the database. Both the data stewards and data custodians who are responsible for data quality work under the strategic direction of the data owner who is accountable for the quality of the data object. Below is an example of data governance on a store master data in a retail company.

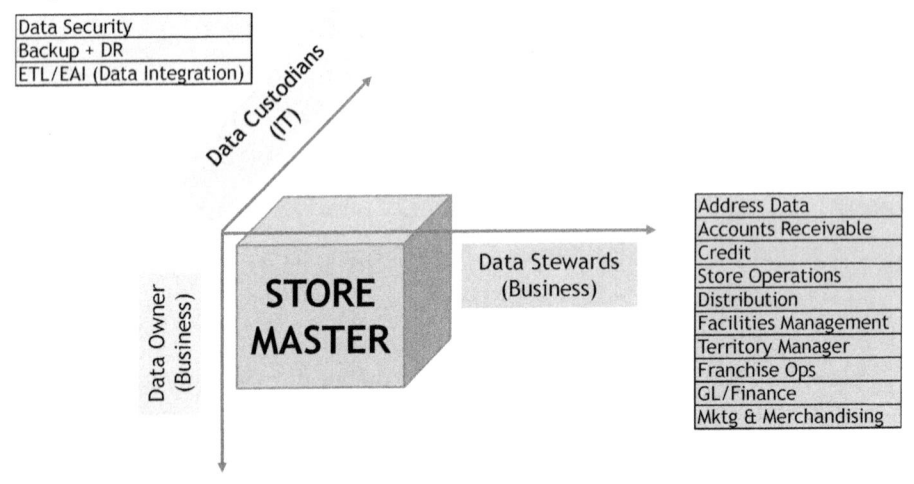

Figure 10.2: Data governance on retail store master data

Set up the process and KPIs to govern these data assets

The third capability in having effective data governance is setting up the processes to govern data assets. Data quality typically degrades over time as businesses are constantly evolving and changing entities. Hence data should be monitored for quality throughout its lifecycle with appropriate KPIs using baselines, thresholds, and targets. Ensuring conformance to those values, and effectively communicating the KPIs to stakeholders will help the business take corrective measures. The data stewards and data custodians should together plan and execute the data governance process that covers the following important aspects:

- The purpose and scope of the data governance program
- Identify the data elements that need to be governed
- Definitions of the roles and the responsibility for the creation, use, retention, archiving and purging of the data assets
- Set up rules for ensuring compliance of data to laws, regulations, business rules, and ethics.
- Define standards for the data quality audits including KPIs for evaluating the success of the data governance program

Conclusion

A good data governance program with consistent processes and responsibilities ensures high data quality. Today data governance is not an option. It helps in risk mitigation as businesses today hold incredible amounts of data about customers, suppliers, prices, products, employees, and more that need to be complied with laws, regulations, industry standards, internal business processes, and ethics. Hence data governance helps businesses to properly and proactively manage data and reduce its financial and compliance liability. This means good quality data, better analytics models, better insights, better business decisions, and ultimately offer superior business results.

References

- DGI, https://bit.ly/33Xv0aq, Jan 2020.
- Gartner, Gartner Glossary, https://gtnr.it/3bIRVsX, 2020.
- Southekal, Prashanth, "Data for Business Performance," Technics Publications, 2017.

CHAPTER 11

Best Practice #10

Implement Insights with Data Storytelling and Change Management

"Those who tell the stories rule society."

Plato

The previous nine best practices focused mainly on deriving insights. But all the hard work involved in deriving insights from data should be communicated well to the stakeholders so that appropriate business actions can be derived using the insights. Unless the insights are communicated and presented effectively for consumption, the data used for analytics, or the sophistication of the analytics models or the complexity of statistical analysis doesn't really matter. So, how can one effectively present the insights? One effective best practice technique is data storytelling.

Data storytelling has been an integral part of humanity for thousands of years. Analysis of the most popular 500 TED talk presentations found that stories made up at least 65% of their content [Dykes, 2016]. Telling stories is more effective because it is more memorable and persuasive than reporting statistics. Chip Heath, a professor at Stanford University, found that when students are asked to recall speeches, 63% remembered the stories, and only 5% remembered any individual statistic. Therefore, the insights gleaned from data should be presented in the form of stories so that those insights can be consumed appropriately.

Fundamentally data storytelling is communicating the insights from data in a structured manner. Based on the work of data visualization expert Stephen Few, storytelling is a combination of four key elements: data, visuals, narrative, and benefits [Few, 2013], and this can help in explaining, enlightening, and engaging the audience. Narrative, when coupled with data helps to **explain** to the audience what is happening in the data and why an insight is important. When visuals (charts and graphs) are applied to data, they can **enlighten** the audience to insights. When narrative and visuals are merged, they can **engage** the audience. Finally, the insights should communicate the **benefits** in a financial manner as the primary goal of a business enterprise is to offer financial returns to its stakeholders.

So, when the right visuals, narrative, data is presented in a manner that offers financial benefits to the business, you have a compelling data story that can drive **change.** So, when it comes time to change and deploy analytics, good change management helps so that the resulting solutions are accepted within the business. The data storytelling framework is as illustrated below.

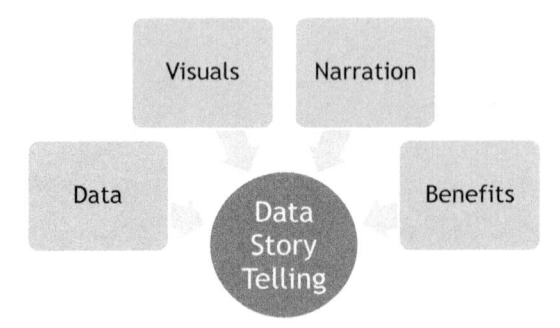

Figure 11.1: Data storytelling components

Data storytelling needs to be integrated with change management in managing and transitioning individuals, teams, and organizations to a desired future state.

Fundamentally, making decisions and taking actions from insights is a combination of data storytelling and change management. According to Robert Schaffer, a world-renowned management consultant, all management is change management [Schaffer, 2017]. Change management happens at the individual level, and the Kubler-Ross change curve helps in understanding how people will respond to change while communicating insights. The five stages of change are shown in Figure 11.2 [Kubler-Ross and Kessler, 2005].

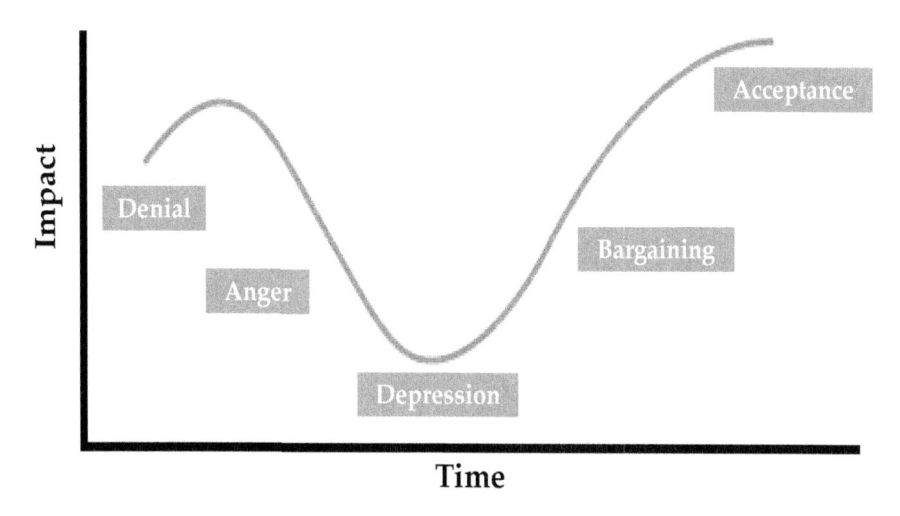

Figure 11.2: Kubler-Ross Change Curve

Why is this a best practice?

Today, an unprecedented amount of data is used for generating insights. These insights must be communicated in a clear way to the business stakeholders so that decisions can be taken. According to Google's Chief Economist, Dr. Hal Varian stated, "The ability to take data, understand it, process it, extract value from it, visualize it, and communicate it—is going to be a hugely important skill in the next decades" [Dykes, 2016]. However, as business data gets bigger and more complex, the ability to tell a compelling story on the insights derived to the business stakeholders becomes more important than ever. According to Tom Davenport, Fellow of the MIT Center for Digital Business, there are four key reasons why data storytelling is important to organizations [Davenport, 2015].

1. Data stories supply context, insight, interpretation—all the things that make data meaningful and analytics more relevant and interesting.

2. No matter how impressive the analysis is, or how high the data quality is, one is not going to compel change unless the stakeholders understand the insights. That may require a visual story or a narrative one, but they require a story.

3. Most people cannot understand the details of analytics, but they do want evidence of analysis and data. Stories that incorporate data and analytics are more convincing than those based on anecdotes.

4. Businesses need the salient findings from an analysis in a brief, snappy way. Stories fit the bill.

While a data story is the first dimension of implementing the insights, change management is the second dimension. Change management is important if the insights need to be consumed for taking action. Change is unsettling for almost every human being. According to Prosci, a well-known change management company, companies with excellent change management are six times more likely to reach their objectives than those with poor change management [Prosci, 2019]. It is, therefore, important for companies to manage change as effectively as possible during the process of data storytelling because managing a successful change can positively affect business productivity.

Realizing the best practice

As discussed earlier, this best practice of implementing insights has two key elements – data storytelling and change management. We will start first on realizing the elements behind data storytelling.

> *The closer you are to your business, the more insight intensive you become.*

Data storytelling

The first best practice in implementing insights is with data storytelling. Data storytelling is communicating the insights from data in a structured way, using a combination of four key elements: data, visuals, narrative, and benefits.

Data in data storytelling

We have discussed the role of data in analytics in the previous chapters. But when telling an effective data story, the business stakeholders need to know three main aspects of data.

1. Relation or the association of data to the problem. For example, if the business objective is on improving the sales performance of the retail store, then the expectation is that key data objects like store data, product data, customer demographic data, and PoS (Point of sale) data were used for analytics.

2. A data source is where the data was extracted and used for deriving insights. The source where the data will be sourced for deriving insights should ideally be the data capture system, that is, the transactional IT system or the data warehouse or data lake system. As discussed in the data governance best practices section – the chances of getting good quality data increased if you are source data from the initial stages of the

data lifecycle. Hence it is better to source data from IT systems that are in the initial stages of the DLC.

3. Key data quality dimensions, such as accuracy, timeliness, security, and privacy. While in Chapter 5, we discussed the 12 data quality dimensions, the important data quality dimensions that matter from the data storytelling perspective are:

    - **Accuracy**. This is the degree to which the data correctly describes the "real world" entities and events.

    - **Timeliness** is the freshness in data. If the analytics is on the sales performance of the retail store, it is imperative that the analytics is done with the most recent data set like the last 12 months or 18 months.

    - **Security and privacy**. This is how the data is extracted and kept secure for analytics. For example, if the data on the sales performance of the retail store includes product margins, it should be secured so that vendors do not get access to the list price of their products.

Visuals in data storytelling

They say that a picture is worth a thousand words. This is because the way the human brain processes information, using charts or graphs is easier than reviewing details over spreadsheets or reports. Data Visuals or Visual Analytics is the pictorial or graphical representation of data. It enables decision-makers to see data and insights visually, so they can grasp difficult concepts or identify new patterns and trends. If the visuals are interactive, one can drill down into charts and graphs for more detail, changing what data to see and how it is processed. Given that analytics is fundamentally using data to answer business questions, data visuals like bar graphs, pie-charts, and scatter charts, can be categorized into four sections: comparison, relationship, distribution, and trends. These four main question categories were mapped to the 13 visuals in the discussion on dashboards in chapter 7.

Persuasive narration in data storytelling

The third key element in data storytelling is persuasive narration. Narration turns a story into the information or knowledge for the recipient. Technically a narrative has five basic elements: the characters, the setting, the plot, the conflict, and the resolution.

1. In business analytics, the **characters** are the consumers of insights who will convert the insights into actions.

2. The **setting** is the location or the environment of the story. In business analytics, this includes the business and analytics drivers, concerns, and threats of the business and its stakeholders.

3. The **plot** is the sequence of events that make up the story. In analytics, it is the methodology on how the goal, problem, and questions were formulated, data selected, algorithms picked, and the insights derived. In this phase, identify emotional drivers as it will help determine what your business stakeholders truly care about. According to Seth Godin, entrepreneur and author, "People do not buy goods and services. They buy relations, stories, and magic." Harvard Business School professor Gerald Zaltman says that 95% of our purchase decision making takes place in the subconscious mind [Zaltman, 2003]. Renowned psychologists Daniel Kahneman and Amos Tversky have shown that humans often make choices that defy clear logic [Tversky and Kahneman, 1974].

4. The fourth dimension in persuasive narration is **conflict**. Every story has a conflict or problem to solve, and in analytics, the conflict is the value

proposition of doing analytics for business insights and results. Value proposition defines the call-to-action—the prompt for immediate response or action based on insights.

5. Finally, the fifth element of narration, **resolution**, is the solution to the problem. It is on how the insights can be used to derive actions for better business performance and results.

Benefits in data storytelling

Finally, the fourth aspect of data storytelling is the financial aspects. That means the value of insights should be presented in financial benefits using three key metrics - NPV (net present value), WACC (weighted average cost of capital), and Return on Invested Capital (ROIC).

- NPV is the difference between the present value of cash inflows and the present value of cash outflows over a period.
- The WACC is the rate that a company is expected to pay its investors. WACC is a metric a company can use to make better decisions on how to allocate their capital. WACC is the average cost of raising capital – equity and debt.
- Lastly, ROIC is the measure of return that investors are earning from the capital invested in the business. The term ROIC and ROI can be used interchangeably.

The NPV is used to calculate ROIC. So, if the ROIC on the analytics initiative is more than the company's WACC, then there is a better chance of getting stakeholder's approval. Below is an example where ROIC is calculated using the cash flow of US$ 5.6, US$ 5.9, and US$ 6.2 million for each of the three years against an investment of US$12.2 million and compared against the WACC of 7.8% to assess the financial viability of the analytics initiative. In this case, the ROIC is 25.4 % indicating that the proposed analytics initiative is highly profitable for the business.

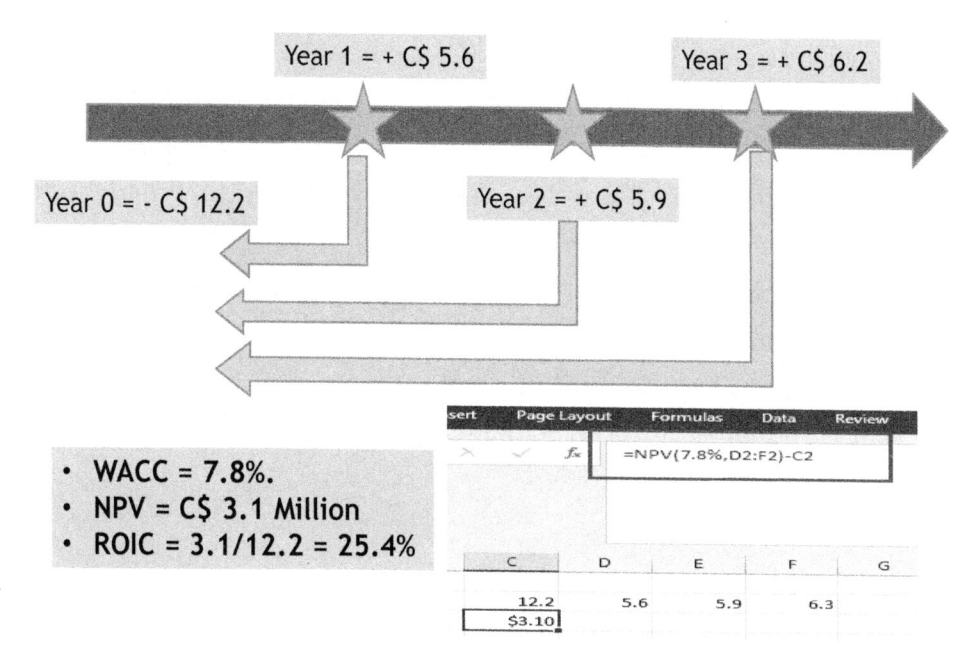

Figure 11.3: ROIC calculation

Change management in analytics

The second key element in implementing insights after data storytelling is effective change management. Successful analytics initiatives require good change management so that the insights are consumed by business stakeholders. The most cited reason for the failure of any business initiatives is the problems with the people side of change. Change management is the discipline that guides how we prepare, equip, and support individuals to successfully adopt change in order to drive organizational outcomes. It includes methods that redirect or redefine the use of resources, business processes, budget allocations, or other modes of operation that significantly change a company or organization.

According to Gartner, the cultural challenges to accept change are the main reason why analytics projects fail [Gartner, 2019]. While many of the change management practices like training and communication are applicable to analytics initiatives, the key change management aspects specific to analytics are linking the insights to the goal, the prevailing KPIs, and the impact of insights on the existing business process. The ADKAR model, which is a goal-oriented change management model, looks at change as a process and not as an event. ADKAR is an acronym that represents the five milestones or outcomes necessary for change to be successful: **a**wareness, **d**esire, **k**nowledge, **a**bility, and **r**einforcement. The three states of change—current state, transition state, and future state—provide a powerful framework for the process-oriented approach of the ADKAR Model.

Conclusion

Analytics initiatives often face confusion and resistance when communicating insights. By adopting the right change management strategies and the four key data storytelling tactics, analytics initiatives can turn resistance into engagement and business results. Unless the data sets and insights are presented well, no one will act on it, and no change will occur. At the same time, data storytelling is not just about communicating insights; sometimes, it is what not to communicate and this requires an understanding of the market, business, and the insight consumers. Ultimately data per se is just a collection of numbers; it must be turned into a story such that data and insights are consumed appropriately.

References

- Abela, V, "Chart Suggestions—A Thought-Starter," https://bit.ly/2WZKpFM, 2009.
- Davenport, Tom, https://bit.ly/2wQZC1k, Jan 2015.

- Dykes, Brent, "Data Storytelling: The Essential Data Science Skill Everyone Needs," https://bit.ly/2WZuzem, Mar 2016.
- Few, Stephen, "Information Dashboard Design: Displaying Data for At-a-Glance Monitoring," Analytics Press, 2013.
- Kubler-Ross, Elisabeth and David Kessler, "On Grief and Grieving: Finding the Meaning of Grief through the Five Stages of Loss," Scribner's & Company, 2005.
- Prosci, https://bit.ly/3atmVNc, 2019.
- Schaffer, Robert, "All Management Is Change Management," Harvard Business Review, Oct 2017.
- Tversky, Amos and Kahneman, Daniel, "Judgment under Uncertainty: Heuristics and Biases," Science, Sep 1974.
- Zaltman, Gerald, "How Customers Think: Essential Insights into the Mind of the Market," Harvard Business School Press, 2003.

CHAPTER 12

Conclusion

"Great things are not done by impulse, but by a series of small things brought together."

Vincent van Gogh

Most business enterprises today are data-rich but poor in insights. For example, the oil and gas industry has historically captured data for operations and compliance, and today they are aggressively building capabilities to convert the captured data to insights [Wethe, 2018]. In transforming data into insights, this book offers practical guidance with these ten key analytics best practices on what one can do for successfully delivering analytics initiatives for the organization:

1. Tie stakeholders' goals to questions and KPIs. This best practice can be realized with:
    - Identify stakeholder's business and analytics goal
    - Strengthening the goal statement with pertinent questions
    - Refining the strengthened goal statement with KPIs.

2. Build a high performing team for analytics. This can be implemented by:
    - Data literacy as the foundation
    - A strong analytics leader such as the CDO
    - Staffing the team across the entire data lifecycle (DLC)
    - Hypothesis-based methodology
    - Execution mechanism for data analytics.

3. Understand the data from the analytics view. Realization of this best practice is with:
    - Profiling the enterprise data
    - Transforming the native state of data into the analytics view
    - Balancing the cost and business value in deriving the analytics data types.

4. Source data strategically. This best practice can be implemented by:
    - Data sampling
    - Feature engineering (FE)
    - Acquiring new data and blending it with existing data.

5. Make data compliance an integral part of analytics. This can be delivered with:
    - Compliance to external and internal mandates
    - Compliance to business purpose
    - Compliance to transparency.

6. Focus on descriptive analytics for data literacy. This can be implemented by:
    - Use data to build the data-driven culture
    - Building data pipelines
    - Implementing reports and dashboards.

7. Use continuous refinement and validation as the mainstay of advanced analytics. This best practice can be realized with:
    - Cross-validation of data
    - Validation of output from multiple algorithms
    - What-if scenarios on the independent variables to optimize business resource utilization.

8. Leverage analytics for data monetization. This best practice can be delivered with:
   - Data architecture
   - Embedded analytics
   - Data products.

9. Support analytics with data governance. Realize this best practice by:
   - Identifying the data assets to be governed
   - Identifying the data owner, data stewards, and data custodians of these data assets
   - Setting up the process and KPIs to govern these data assets.

10. Implement insights for business results. This can be implemented by:
    - Data storytelling
    - Change management.

These ten best analytics practices were applied in an analytics program in an OFS (Oil Field Services) company. The first section of this chapter will share details on how these best practices were applied in this OFS company. Also, throughout the book, the discussion was focused on delivering good analytics and insights. If successful analytics depends on senior management support, stakeholder alignment, data architecture, quality data, the right algorithms, and change management, how does bad analytics look? The second section of this chapter is on bad analytics. Lastly, deriving insights rely on the statistical models. So, what are the key statistical tools required to derive business insights? In all, this chapter looks at three main topics – a case study, what bad analytics looks like, and the key statistical tools for analytics.

Before we look at these three topics, Figure 12.1 summarizes the different types of business analytics discussed so far.

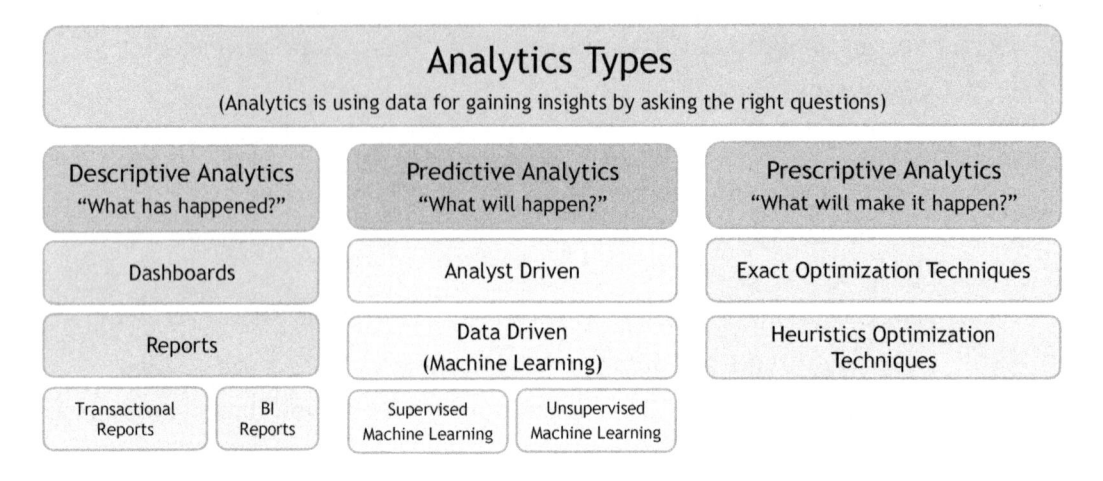

Figure 12.1: Analytics taxonomy

Case study: Data insight product for Payload Technologies

The ten best analytics practices discussed in the previous chapters were implemented in Payload (PL) Technologies (https://www.payload.com/), a Canadian Oil Field Services (OFS) technology company based in Calgary, Canada. Payload has two flagship cloud SaaS (Software-as-a-Service) products – eTicket and eManifest. These two products, which are used for digitizing oil movement regulatory documents, can be accessed as a web application or as a mobile application.

- The Oil and Gas Exploration and Production (E&P) regulatory process requires the E&P companies to use work orders, and Bills-of-lading (BoL) for tracking oil transportation, and this document is called a field ticket. Field ticket, which is a requirement of the provincial regulator, is managed in eTicket to capture details such as a product type, volume, and the pickup and the drop off locations.

- eManifests are digital work order and BoL documents required for submission to the energy regulator on the transportation of dangerous substances like oil as per the requirements of Federal Transportation of Dangerous Goods (TDG) regulations of Transport Canada.

Payload's current operating model is a digital network platform. A digital network platform is a technology-enabled business model that creates value by facilitating interactions between two or more interdependent groups. Technically, digital platforms have three distinct features.

- Firstly, the network effect brings together users to create transactions.
- Secondly, digital platforms enable concurrence of technologies—cloud, analytics and mobile to create more services
- Thirdly, digital platforms enable easy data access using APIs to derive more insights

Payload's digital network platform is as shown below. In Payload's digital network platform, there are three interdependent groups – the E&P companies, the trucking companies, and the drivers. The E&P companies search for oil reserves and then drill the oil wells to extract oil. Once the oil is extracted, the oil products are transported by the trucking companies from the oil wells to the collection points for further shipments to the refineries. In Payload's digital network platform, there are seven E&P companies that have contracted over 120 trucking companies who work with over 1900 drivers for the oil product movement.

In this backdrop, Payload (PL) has captured operational and compliance data on oil movements for over five years from the E&P companies, trucking companies, and the drivers. This data is approximately 425,000 field tickets and manifests that cover transportation of about 65 million barrels of crude oil (and it's derivative products like emulsion and condensate) over 86 million kilometers resulting in a trade of over C$ 3.5 billion for the Canadian Oil industry.

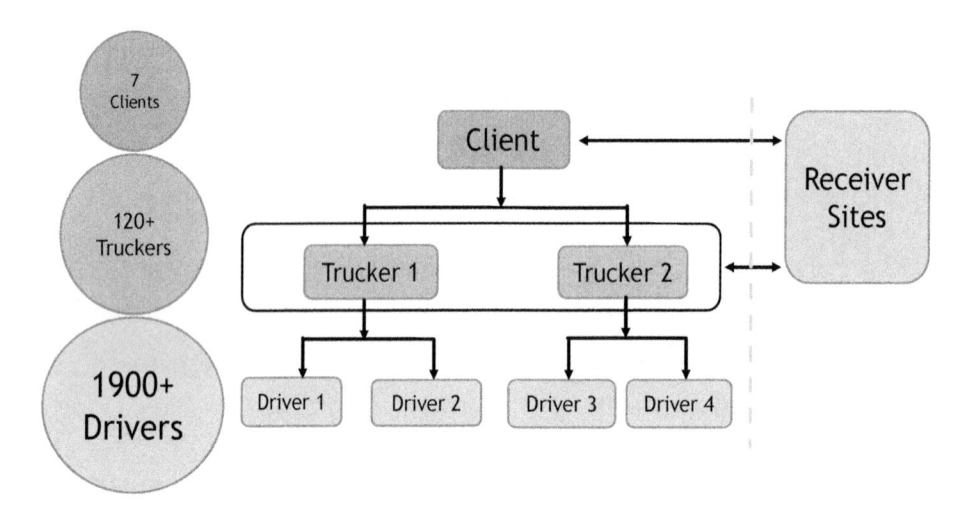

Figure 12.2: Digital network platform of Payload

Payload wants to monetize the data and offer insights to the E&P and the Trucking companies as a new data analytics product. The data product will be valuable to these companies as these data products will give them insights to:

- Reduce Operational Risk
- Identify Value Leaks and
- Predict the Cash Flow, payables for the E&P and receivables, for the trucking companies

The business operating model, that is, value stream mapping (VSM), of Payload (PL), is mapped to create the enterprise data model (EDM). The EDM shown below is based on the conceptual and integrated value chain of four key elements – Projects, Orders, Field tickets, and Master Tickets and uses different types of reference data, master data, and transactional data elements.

As the first step in building the new data product, the Payload analytics team identified the stakeholder personas and their key value proposition, basically tied the stakeholders' goals to questions & KPIs.

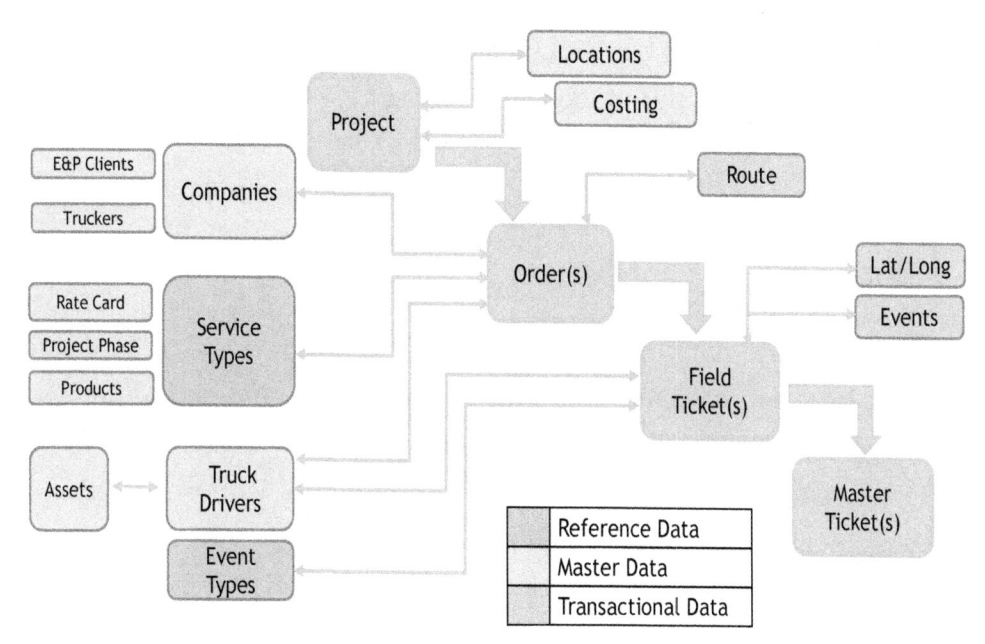

Figure 12.3: Payload conceptual data model

#	Organizations	Stakeholder Personas	Business Drivers and KPIs
1	E&P Companies	Logistics Coordinator	• Reliable Service from Trucking companies • Reduced Cost of Oil transportation • Environmental consciousness and Improved Safety
2	Trucking Companies	Dispatcher	• Improved Operating Margins • Environmental consciousness • Regulatory compliance and Safety
3	Drivers	Driver	• Reduced Redirects • Increased Revenue • Improved Safety

Based on the value proposition of the stakeholders, the analytics team worked on addressing the following key business questions:

1. What to move? Is the product oil, emulsion, water, or condensate?
2. How to move? Is the oil movement using a 7-axle truck with 30 M3 capacity or a 5-axle truck with 20 M3 capacity?
3. Where to move? What are the pick-up and destination points?
4. Under what conditions will the oil product be moved?
5. What is the price charged to move the oil products?

The answers or the data related to these key questions were captured in the eTicket and eManifest application and the data was stored in PostgreSQL, an open-source relational database management system. The data from PostgreSQL was transferred every hour to the Snowflake Cloud Data Platform (CDP), which served as the Data warehouse for reporting. As the data was captured in the eTicket and eManifest application in a structured format with data integrity rules, the data quality level was high. Hence, the entire population data set was considered for analytics.

After extensive discussion with Payload's senior management and key subject matter experts (SMEs), the data product strategy was to build the following five analytics offerings. The five data products branded as *PL Insights* are:

1. Basic Data Products for the Trucking Companies
2. Basic Data Products for the E&P Companies
3. Advanced Data Products for the Trucking Companies
4. Advanced Data Products for the E&P Companies
5. Data Products for Oil/Gas Industry

The roadmap for deploying these data products, *PL Insights*, was mapped to the three types of data products, data enhancing, data exchanging, and data experiencing products, as shown in Figure 12.4. The first wave of data product development was to focus on the two data experiencing products - *Basic Data Products for the Trucking Companies* and *Basic Data Products for the E&P Companies*. The priority was to first improve the data literacy and adoption in the user ecosystem or in the digital network with descriptive analytics (reports and dashboard) before embarking on advanced analytics solutions, which were predictive and prescriptive analytics solutions. Hence the development of the data exchanging and data enhancing products was deferred until market success was realized with two basic data analytics products.

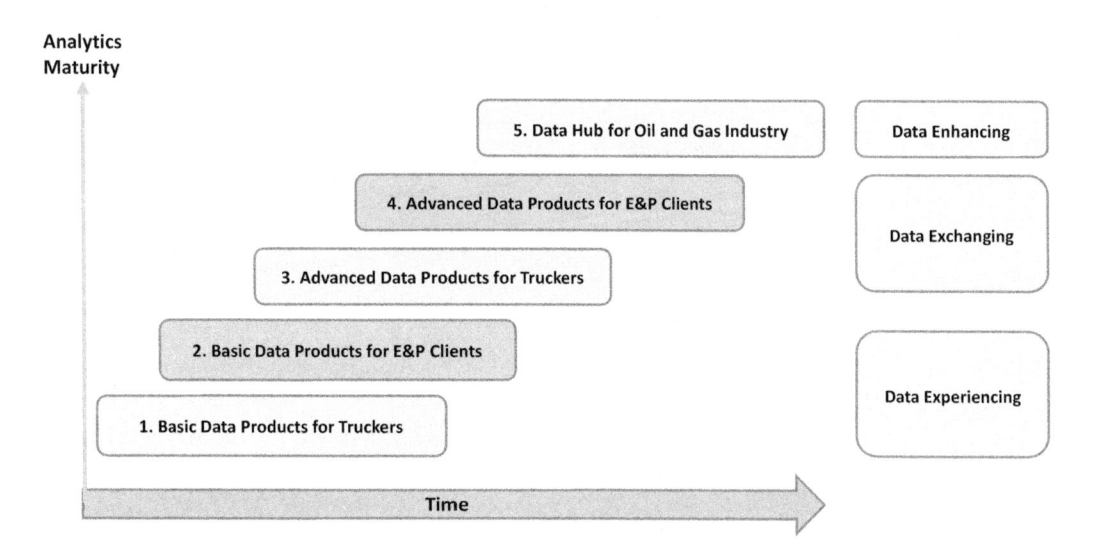

Figure 12.4: Data product roadmap

Basic data analytics products include dashboards and reports. While the reports can be transactional or BI reports, the analytics team blended the key features of transactional and BI reports leveraging the technical capability in the Snowflake data warehouse (DWH) platform. Snowflake data warehouse uses a columnar format to store data and is designed for quick analytic queries. These queries are saved as views and embedded into the eTicket and eManifest products using Sigma Computing, a cloud data analysis and visualization software.

166 • Analytics Best Practices

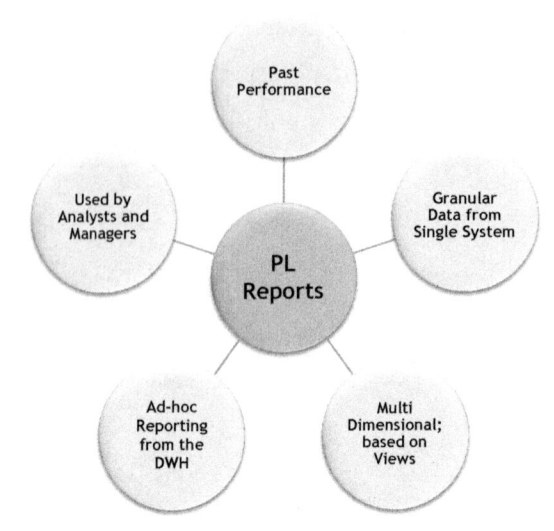

Figure 12.5: Report features in data product

(Central node: PL Reports; surrounding nodes: Past Performance; Granular Data from Single System; Multi Dimensional; based on Views; Ad-hoc Reporting from the DWH; Used by Analysts and Managers)

The Basic Data Product for the Trucking companies appears in Figure 12.6, and for E&P companies in Figure 12.7.

Dashboard Product

#	KPI	UoM
1	Field Ticket Count (Today's Ticket)	
2	Volume Moved in M3	M3
3	Distance Covered in Kms	Kms
4	Driving Time Taken	Hours
5	$ involved in Transportation	Dollars
6	Hazardous Driving Instances	
7	Master Ticket Count	

Basic Reports Product

#	Performance Report
1	Fleet Load Utilization
2	Carbon Footprint
3	Force Quit
4	Driving Violations
5	Driver HoS
6	Truck Load Utilization
7	Field Tickets per Drivers
8	Outlier Tickets
9	Daily Ticket Export
10	Moving Time Breakdowns
11	Field Tickets Disputes Register
12	FT Costs Breakdown
13	Cost over Service Type
14	Monthly Movement Costs

Figure 12.6: Basic data product for trucker companies

Dashboard Product			Basic Reports Product	
#	KPI	UoM	#	Report Name
1	Field Ticket Count (Today's Ticket)		1	Location Activity Map
2	Volume Moved in M3	M3	2	Audit Report
3	Distance Covered in Kms	Kms	3	Volume (BS&W Cubes) Hauled
4	Driving Time Taken	Hours	4	Cost/Service Type (Aggregate)
5	$ involved in Transportation	Dollars	5	Cost/AFE or GL
6	Hazardous Driving Instances		6	Invoiced Amount (Aggregate)
7	Master Ticket Count		7	FT/Vendor
			8	Orders/FT Report
			9	FT Time Breakdowns
			10	FT Costs Breakdown
			11	Outlier Report
			12	Daily Ticket Export (Aggregate)
			13	Mastered and Unmastered Tickets
			14	Field Tickets Disputes Register
			15	FT-MT Reconciliation
			16	Carbon Footprint
Financials Projections			17	Load Utilization
			18	Driving Violations

Figure 12.7: Basic data product for E&P companies

To help Trucking and E&P companies succeed in consuming these data products in their business operations, *PL Insights* was delivered as a holistic solution – a combination of data products and services. While the basic data products for the Trucking and E&P companies included the dashboard and the descriptive analytics reports, the services included:

- Operations Support (7 AM to 10 PM MST, 365 days)
- Training videos and manuals on running the reports and dashboards and interpreting the insights
- FAQs (Frequently Asked Questions)

The data governance was mainly done by the Operations team in Payload. The data governance activities include training the users from the E&P and the trucking companies on using the right descriptive analytics solution, that is, the dashboard and report, assigning the users to the right reports based on RBAC (Role-Based Access Control), data cleansing and validation, and so on.

About bad analytics

While there are a lot of discussions on good analytics, how does bad analytics look? What exactly is bad analytics, and what are its key characteristics? Bad analytics is more than not having good insights. Here are the eleven key characteristics of bad analytics, which will help you identify and prevent bad analytics in your company.

1. Fundamentally, analytics is using data to answer business questions. If the analytics does not answer the QUESTIONS for deriving the insights, the insights have NOT clearly addressed the business objectives, that is, the problem or the opportunity.

2. Bad analytics have insights prone to biases. Bias refers to the tendency to over or underestimate the insights derived. This results in the insights being skewed in a certain direction. Insights can be biased due to:

    a) **Confirmation bias**. A confirmation bias involves favoring insights that confirms previously existing beliefs or findings. It is insights that are already proven or known.
    b) **Availability bias**. Getting good quality data for analytics is challenging. Availability bias is the tendency to share insights that come readily to mind instead of thoroughly analyzing the issue.
    c) **Selection bias**. Selection bias refers to the data sample that does not represent the size of the population. In addition, the sample data is not representative of the population, and there is no proper randomization of the selected data.
    d) **Anchoring bias**. It is fixating on initial information and failing to adapt for subsequent information. This becomes an important issue if the analytics is not made on the most recent data.

e) **Framing bias**. It is the tendency to be influenced by the way a problem is formulated or defined to suit one interests.

f) **Sunk Costs bias**. It is the tendency to "honor" already spent resources, especially time and money. This happens when investments are on bad insights, and businesses do not want to lose the time or money already invested, instead of making the decision that would give them the best outcome going forward.

g) **Authority bias**. Authority bias is accepting the opinion of the highest-paid person's opinion (HiPPO). The highest-paid person usually has the most power and the highest designation in the room. Once his or her opinion is out, dissent is shut out, thereby affecting a thorough analysis of the problem and the solution.

3. Bad analytics is insights derived using poor DATA QUALITY. Often it is very difficult for businesses to get quality data for analytics. The "Garbage-in; Garbage-out" concept is very much applicable for analytics. If the quality of data used in analytics is poor, the insights will also be of bad quality

4. If NON-NORMALIZED DATA is used for business insights, then it is bad analytics. Business processes inherently follow the normalized bell-curve, and if there are any exceptions, businesses will fix these variations as they despise inconsistency. Business processes that capture discrete and continuous events are shown to fit a normal distribution.

5. OUTLIERS. Outliers are observations that are not following the same pattern as the other data sets. Outliers are not necessarily a bad thing all the time in business, as fraud analytics is heavily dependent on outliers. If the outliers are not identified and explained, then it is bad analytics. And if the outliers are eliminated, one should try to understand why

they appeared and whether it is likely similar values will continue to appear.

6. OVERFITTING AND UNDERFITTING. Underfitting means the analytics model gives a simplistic picture of reality, and overfitting is when the model is overcomplicated. Bad analytics is one where the analytics model is not validated with cross-validation (with training and test data) and multiple algorithms.

7. Bad analytics present a CONFOUND variable(s) in the analytics model explaining the insight. A confounding variable(s) is an "extra" variable that is not accounted for analytics. In other words, confounding variables are extra independent variables that are having a hidden effect on the dependent variables.

8. MIXING Correlation and Causation. Correlation describes the relationship between two variables, while causation speaks to the idea that one event is the result of the occurrence of the other event. It is common to assume causation when there is simply a correlation in the data, and this typically happens when individuals working on the data are influenced by experience and personal biases.

9. If the insights derived are OBVIOUS or have high validity, then we have bad analytics. In other words, analytics is solving a problem based on testable hypotheses using good quality data. Spending time in reconfirming an obvious insight is a waste of business resources. For example, if a crude oil pipeline company after analyzing thousands of crude oil nomination tickets determines that crude oil viscosity affects the crude oil transportation time, it is not new insights. In other words, it is bad analytics as it is "solving" a physics problem and not a data problem.

10. The insights are not MONETIZABLE. If the insights derived are not increasing revenue, reducing cost, and minimizing the risk for the business, then we have bad analytics.

11. The insights coming out of bad analytics cannot be implemented with the available RESOURCES. Securing new or additional resources for business is always a challenge. If the insights derived cannot be implemented with the available resources, the insights derived are not very useful.

Overall bad analytics does not support evidence-based and data-driven decision-making (3DM) for business results. Analytics should be designed for a purpose, and the best way to avoid bad analytics is to work on real problems for actual customers or stakeholders. In other words, tying stakeholder insight needs to goals, questions, and quality data.

Selecting statistical tools for analytics

The decision of which statistical test to use depends on the business question, the distribution of the data, and the data type of the variable. As discussed in Chapter 11, there are four main types of business questions from a statistical perspective – composition, comparison, relationship, and distribution. The business data is normally distributed and hence parametric tests are used. In general, if the data is normally distributed, parametric tests should be used. The data type of the analytics variable is nominal, ordinal and continuous. The image below is a list of key statistical tests and their typical use cases.

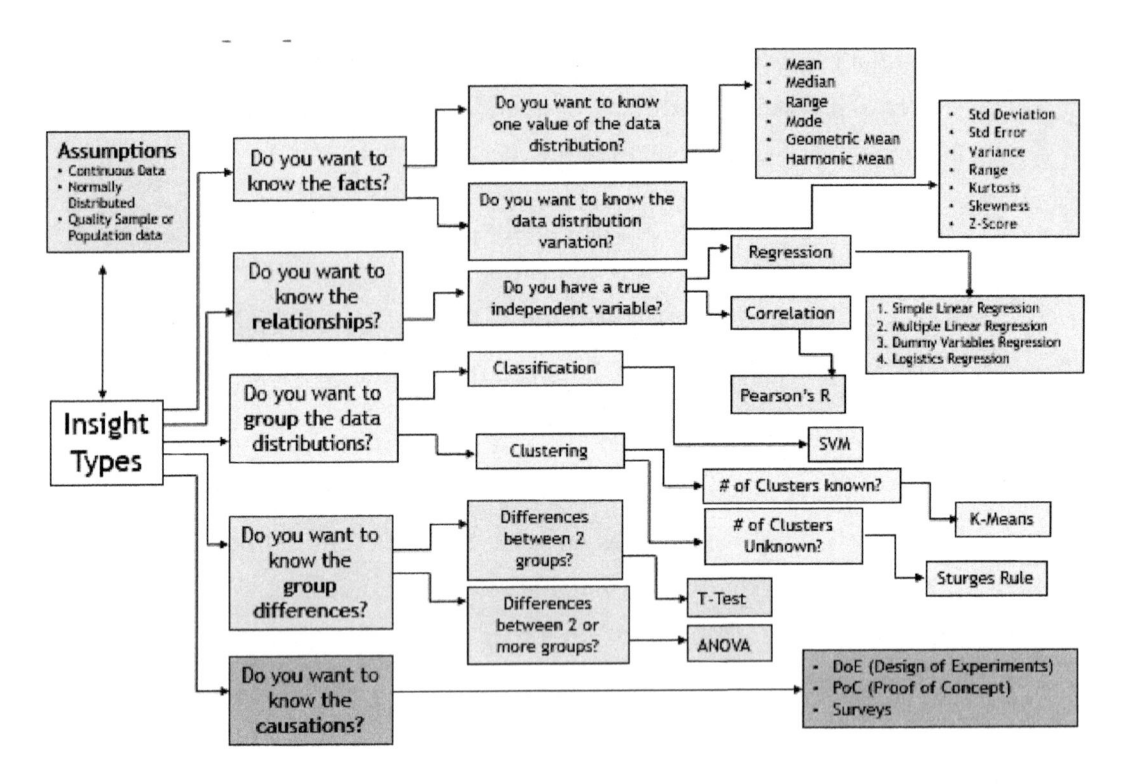

Figure 12.8: Statistical tool selection flow chart for generating insights

Closing thoughts

The amount of data generated by the business today is unprecedented. As this growth continues, so do the opportunities for organizations to derive insights from their data analytics initiatives and derive sustainable competitive advantage. Given the complexity in business operations, today, decision making must inevitably rely on the insights derived from data analytics. Analytics today is seen as the next frontier for innovation and productivity in business. But achieving a sustainable competitive advantage from analytics is a complex endeavor and demands a lot of commitment from the organization.

As discussed in chapter 1, the implementation of these ten best analytics practices is in a playbook fashion – a combination of strategy and tactical elements to deliver the greatest value to the business. From the strategic perspective, it means enabling organizations to develop the analytics talent, the culture, data literacy, the discipline, and the organization structure. From a tactical perspective, it means implementation of the ten best analytics practices that reflects the process workflows, standard operating procedures (SOP), and the cultural values.

In implementing the ten best practices, the analytic team will run into many challenges. If there is no data or quality data for validating the hypothesis, one option is to rework your hypothesis. If the team is challenged with acquiring data internally, one approach is to get data from external sources. If there is no good data for analytics, one strategy is to leverage sampling or feature engineering techniques. If there is no precise or accurate business data, one solution is to use ranges and confidence intervals. The bottom line is that analytics is a probabilistic process and not a deterministic process. One cannot expect a perfect situation in the analytics initiatives. It simply doesn't exist. Overall, the analytics implementation is an evolutionary process, just like the business entity itself. The insight needs of the businesses constantly change, the organizational capabilities continuously mature, the data sets grow, improve, and sometimes even degrade, and the technological capabilities to process the data improve over time.

Reference

- Wethe, David, "'Netflix for Oil' Setting Stage for $1 Trillion Battle Over Data," https://bit.ly/2WYDY5O, Mar 2018.

Appendix 1

Data Quality Dimensions

The 12 dimensions of data quality that are applicable to business performance are listed below.

1. **Completeness (or Entirety).** Completeness is the degree of usage of the attributes of a specific data element. This is ensuring that no key field is left populated.

2. **Consistency.** Consistency means that data values for a specific data element within the enterprise system landscape are the same. For example, the GL account for customer deposits in the CRM system should have the same value in the ERP system as well.

3. **Conformity (Validity).** Conformity, also known as validity, refers to data that adheres to specifications, standards, or guidelines, including data type, description, size, format, and other characteristics.

4. **Uniqueness (Cardinality).** Uniqueness, also called cardinality, points out that there are no duplicates values for a data element.

5. **Correctness.** Closely related to accuracy is correctness. Correctness is freedom from error or mistakes. It is Boolean; something is either correct or not, and there cannot be a degree of correctness. A customer's bank account number needs to be correct; even a mistake of one character is not acceptable.

6. **Accuracy.** Accuracy is the degree to which data truly reflects the business category, entity, or event. Correctness and accuracy go together.

For example, the supplier's phone number needs to be correct, while the supplier's name needs to be accurate.

7. **Accessibility.** Data accessibility refers to how easy (or not) it is to access or retrieve data within a database in the system.

8. **Security.** Data security is protecting data from unauthorized users or systems.

9. **Currency (Timeliness).** Fundamentally, data quality is time-sensitive; data values continuously change during the data lifecycle. Currency (or "freshness") refers to how "stale" the data is, and how much time has elapsed since it was created or last changed. For example, if vendor payment terms have not been updated for years, the data involved would be termed low-quality, as there could be a potential opportunity to renegotiate the contracts with the vendor for better deals.

10. **Redundancy.** Data redundancy is a condition created within a database or data storage technology in which the data element is replicated and captured by two separate IT systems in two different locations for backup and recovery purposes.

11. **Coverage.** Data coverage is the extent to which data is shared. Reference data (on business categories) and master data (on business entities) have high coverage as they are usually shared in the enterprise, while transactional data has less data coverage as they are specific to one LoB or business function or business event.

12. **Integrity.** Data integrity includes ensuring that data is recorded exactly as intended and that when data is retrieved, it is the same as it was when originally recorded.

APPENDIX 2

Analytics Abbreviations and Acronyms

- 3DM – Data-Driven Decision Making
- AI – Artificial Intelligence
- ACID - Atomicity, Consistency, Isolation, and Durability
- ADKAR - Awareness, Desire, Knowledge, Ability, and Reinforcement
- ANSI - American National Standards Institute
- API - Application Programming Interface
- ARIMA - AutoRegressive Integrated Moving Average
- ARTS - Association for Retail Technology Standards
- B2C - Business to Consumer
- BA - Business Analytics
- BI - Business Intelligence
- BP – Best Practice
- CART - Classification and Regression Trees
- CCPA - California Consumer Privacy Act
- CDO - Chief Data Officer
- COBIT - Control Objectives for Information and Related Technologies
- CoD – Cost of Delay
- COTS - Commercial-off-the-shelf
- CRM - Customer Relationship Management
- CRUD: Create, Read, Update, and Delete
- D&A - Data and Analytics
- DAM – Digital Asset Management
- DBMS - Database Management System
- DLC – Data Lifecycle
- DM – Data Monetization

- EAI - Enterprise Application Integration
- EDA - Exploratory Data Analysis,
- EDG - Enterprise Data Governance
- EDM – Enterprise Data Model
- EDIFACT - Electronic Data Interchange for Administration, Commerce, and Transport
- ERP - Enterprise Resource Planning
- ETL - Extract, Transform, and Load
- FAAMG - Facebook, Amazon, Apple, Microsoft, and Google
- FK – Foreign Key
- FMV - Fair Market Value
- GAAP - Generally Accepted Accounting Principles
- GDPR - General Data Protection Regulation
- HIPAA - Health Insurance Portability and Accountability Act
- IDM - Identity Management
- IFRS - International Financial Reporting Standards
- ISO - International Organization for Standardization
- IT - Information Technology
- IoT - Internet of Things
- KPI - Key Performance Indicator
- LoB - Line of Business
- LMA – Last Mile Analytics
- MAD- Monitor, Analyze, Detect
- MCCE - Mutually Exclusive and Collectively Exhaustive
- MD&A - Management Discussion and Analysis
- MDM - Master Data Management
- ML - Machine Learning
- MLR – Multiple Linear Regression
- NACS - National Association of Convenience Stores
- NLP – Natural Language Processing

- NPV – Net Present Value
- OLTP - Online Transaction Processing
- OLAP - Online Analytical Processing
- PCI DSS - Payment Card Industry Data Security Standard
- PIDX - Petroleum Industry Data Exchange
- PII - Personally Identifiable Information
- PIPEDA - Personal Information Protection and Electronic Documents Act of Canada
- PDPA - Personal Data Protection Act of Singapore
- PIDX - Petroleum Industry Data Exchange
- PoC – Proof of Concept
- PoS - Point of Sale
- PK – Primary Key
- PLM - Product Lifecycle Management
- RBAC – Role-Based Access Control
- RBF – Resource-Based Framework
- ROIC - Return on Investment Capital
- SaaS - Software-as-a-Service
- SCADA - Supervisory Control And Data Acquisition
- SIN - Social Insurance Number
- SoI - System of Insights
- SoR - System of Record
- SCA – Sustainable Competitive Advantage
- SOX – Sarbanes -Oxley Act
- SQL - Structured Query Language
- SSA – Self Serve Analytics
- SVM – Support Vector Machine
- TCO - Total Cost of Ownership
- TDWI - The Data Warehousing Institute
- TOGAF - The Open Group Architecture Framework

- UNSPSC - United Nations Standard Products and Services Code
- UPC - Universal Product Code
- VSM – Value Stream Mapping
- WACC – Weighted Average Cost of Capital

Appendix 3

Analytics Glossary

- **ACID Test:** A test applied to data for atomicity, consistency, isolation, and durability.

- **Aggregation:** A process of searching, gathering, and presenting data.

- **Algorithm:** A mathematical formula or statistical process used to perform analysis of data.

- **API (Application Program Interface)**: A set of programming standards and instructions for accessing or building web-based software applications.

- **Artificial Intelligence**: The ability of a machine to apply information gained from previous experience accurately to new situations in a way that a human would.

- **Best Practice:** A best practice is a guideline or idea that has been generally accepted as superior to any alternatives because it produces results that are prescriptive, superior, and reusable.

- **Big Data**: Big data refers to datasets whose size is beyond the ability of typical database software tools to capture, store, manage, and analyze. Big data sets are characterized by 3Vs: volume, velocity, and variety.

- **Business Intelligence**: The general term used for the identification, extraction, and analysis of multi-dimensional data.

- **CDO 4.0.** According to Gartner, with the increased usage of data and analytics (D&A) across the enterprise, the chief data officer's (CDO) focus needs to shift from focusing on D&A projects and programs to products.

- o   CDO 1.0 was focused exclusively on data management.
- o   CDO 2.0 started to embrace analytics.
- o   CDO 3.0 led and participated quite heavily in digital transformation.
- o   CDO 4.0 is focused on data products

- **Change Management:** Change management is the discipline that guides how we prepare, equip, and support individuals to successfully adopt change in order to drive organizational success and outcomes.

- **Cloud Computing**: A distributed computing system hosted and running on remote servers and accessible from anywhere on the internet.

- **Correlation.** Correlation is a statistical technique that shows how strongly two variables are related. For example, height and weight are correlated; taller people tend to be heavier than shorter people.

- **Cube.** A data structure in OLAP systems. It is a method of storing data in a multidimensional form, generally for reporting purposes. In OLAP cubes, data (measures) are categorized by dimensions. OLAP cubes are often pre-summarized across dimensions to drastically improve query time over relational databases

- **Dashboard**: A graphical representation of KPIs and Visuals.

- **Data**: Data is a set of fields with quantitative or qualitative values in a specific format.

- **Data Analyst**: A person responsible for the tasks of modeling, preparing and cleaning data for the purpose of deriving actionable information from it.

- **Data Analytics**: The process of answering business questions using data. Businesses typically use the three types of analytics: *Descriptive, Predictive and Prescriptive Analytics.*

- **Data Architecture**: It is the mechanism in which data is collected, and how it is stored, arranged, integrated, and put to use in data systems and in organizations.

- **Data Broker:** Data broker is a data product that aggregates data from a variety of sources, processes it, enriches it, cleanse or analyzes it, and licenses it to other organizations as data products.

- **Data Center:** A data center is a dedicated space used to house computer systems and associated components, such as telecommunications and storage systems.

- **Data Cleansing**: The process of reviewing and revising data to delete duplicate entries, correct misspelling and other errors, add missing data, and provide consistency.

- **Data Governance**: A set of processes or rules that ensure data integrity and data management best practices are met.

- **Data Integration**: The process of combining data from different sources and presenting it in a single view.

- **Data Hub:** A data hub is a collection of data from multiple sources organized for distribution and sharing. Generally, this data distribution and sharing is in the form of a hub and spoke architecture.

- **Data Integrity**: The measure of trust an organization has in the accuracy, completeness, timeliness, and validity of the data.

- **Data Lake**: A large repository of enterprise-wide data in raw format – structured and unstructured data.

- **Data Mart**: The access layer of a data warehouse used to provide data to users.

- **Data Mining**: It is finding meaningful patterns and deriving insights in large sets of data using sophisticated pattern recognition techniques. To derive meaningful patterns, data miners use statistics, machine learning algorithms, and artificial intelligence techniques.

- **Data Product**: A data product is the application of data for improving business performance; it is usually an output of the data science activity.

- **Data Science**: A discipline that incorporates statistics, data visualization, computer programming, data mining, machine learning, and database engineering to solve complex problems.

- **Data Storytelling:** Data storytelling is communicating the insights from data using a combination of four key elements: data, visuals, narrative, and benefits.

- **Data Warehouse**: A repository for enterprise-wide data but in a structured format after cleaning and integrating with other sources. Data warehouses are typically used for conventional data (but not exclusively).

- **Database**: A digital collection of data and the structure around which the data is organized. The data is typically entered into and accessed via a database management system.

- **Descriptive Analytics:** Condensing big numbers into smaller pieces of information. This is like summarizing the data story. Rather than listing every single number and detail, there is a general thrust and narrative.

- **Digital Asset Management (DAM):** DAM is a system that stores, shares, and organizes digital assets in a central location

- **Digital Vortex.** The Digital Vortex is the inevitable movement of industries toward a "digital center" in which business models, offerings, and value chains are digitized to the maximum extent possible.

- **Discrete Data**: Data that is not measured on a continuous scale. Also known as intermittent data. Discrete data is based on counts.

- **ETL (Extract, Transform and Load)**: The process of extracting raw data, transforming by cleaning/enriching the data to make it fit operational needs and loading into the appropriate repository for the system's use.

- **Event**: A set of outcomes of an experiment (a subset of the sample space) to which a probability is assigned.

- **Exploratory Analysis**: An approach to data analysis focused on identifying general patterns in data, including outliers and features of the data.

- **Feature Engineering**: It is creating a "smarter" dataset or attributes or features applying the domain experience, and intuition on the existent data sets. Basically, feature engineering serves two main purposes: Transform data types and Create new fields or attributes.

- **Hypothesis.** A hypothesis is an assumption, an idea, or a gut feeling that is proposed for the validation so that it can be tested to see if it might be true.

- **IoT (Internet of Things)**: The network of physical objects or "things" embedded with electronics, software, sensors, and connectivity to enable it to achieve greater value and service by exchanging data with the manufacturer, operator and/or other connected devices.

- **Industry 4.0.** The fourth industrial revolution, referred to as Industry 4.0, is geared towards automation and data exchange using cyber-physical systems (CPS), the internet of things (IoT), industrial internet of things (IIOT), cloud computing, cognitive computing, and artificial intelligence (AI).

- **Insight.** It is the understanding of a specific cause and effect within a specific context. In this book, the terms insight and information are used interchangeably.

- **Join:** A data join is when two or more data sets are combined using at least one common column in each data set. Join differs from a union which puts data sets on top of each other, requiring all of the columns to be the same

- **KPI.** A Key Performance Indicator (KPI) is a measurable value that demonstrates how effectively the entity is achieving key objectives or targets.

- **Last Mile Analytics.** LMA is delivering analytics solution by focusing on the last mile of analytics, insight derivation and decision making, throughout the analytics process thereby providing value to the enterprise

- **Linear Regression:** It is the model of the relationship between one scalar response (or dependent variable) and one or more explanatory variables (or independent variables). If there is one explanatory variable, it is called simple linear regression. If there are multiple explanatory variables, it is called multiple linear regression (MLR).

- **Logistic Regression:** Investigates the relationship between response (Y's) and one or more predictors (X's) where Y's are categorical, not continuous, and X's can be either continuous or categorical.

- **MAD Framework:** MAD, which stands for Monitor-Analyze-Detail, is a top-down analysis framework that delivers insights to users based on their needs, thus optimizing adoption and usability.

- **Machine-generated Data:** Data automatically created by machines via sensors or algorithms or any other non-human source. Commonly known as IoT data.

- **Machine Learning:** A method of designing systems that can learn, adjust and improve based on the data fed to them. Using statistical algorithms that are fed to these machines, they learn and continually zero in on "correct" behavior and insights, and they keep improving as more data flows through the system.

- **Master Data.** Master data describe the core entities of the enterprise, like customers, products, suppliers, assets, and so on.

- **Master data management (MDM.** Master data is any non-transactional data that is critical to the operation of a business — for example, customer or supplier data, product information, or employee data. MDM is the process of managing that data to ensure consistency, quality, and availability.

- **Metadata.** Any data used to describe other data — for example, a data file's size or date of creation.

- **Multicollinearity.** It is a state of very high intercorrelations among the independent variables indicating that there are duplicate or redundant variables in the analysis. It is, therefore, a type of disturbance in the data, and if present in the dataset, the insights derived may not be reliable.

- **Normalization.** It is a database design technique that organizes database tables in a manner that reduces redundancy and dependency of data. It divides larger database tables to smaller tables and links them using relationships.

- **Normal Distribution**: Normal distribution, also known as the Gaussian distribution, is a probability distribution that is symmetric about the mean, showing that data near the mean are more frequent in occurrence than data far from the mean. The normal distribution is the familiar bell curve.

- **Online analytical processing (OLAP).** The process of analyzing multidimensional data using three operations: consolidation (the aggregation of available), drill-down (the ability for users to see the underlying details), and slice and dice (the ability for users to select subsets and view them from different perspectives). OLAP systems are used in BI reports.

- **Online transactional processing (OLTP).** The process of providing users with access to large amounts of transactional data in a way that they can derive meaning from it. OLTP systems are used in Transactional reports

- **Predictive Analytics:** Using statistical functions on one or more data sets to predict trends or future events.

- **Prescriptive Analytics:** Prescriptive analytics builds on predictive analytics by including actions and make data-driven decisions by looking at the impacts of various actions.

- **Population**: A dataset that consists of all the members of some group.

- **Reference Data.** Data that reflects the business categories.

- **Regression Analysis**: A modeling technique used to define the association between variables. It assumes a one-way causal effect from predictor variables (independent variables) to a response of another variable (dependent variable). Regression can be used to explain the past and predict future events.

- **SQL (Structured Query Language)**: A programming language for retrieving data from a relational database.

- **SVM.** Support-vector machine (SVM) is a machine learning (ML) algorithm used for data classification.

- **Sample**. A sample data set consists of only a portion of the data from the population.

- **Stored procedure.** A stored procedure is a group of SQL statements that have been created and stored in the database, so it can be reused and shared by multiple programs.

- **Systems of Insight (SoI).** It is the system used to perform data analysis from the data that is combined from the SoR or transactional systems

- **System of Record (SoR).** The authoritative data source for a data element. To ensure data integrity in the enterprise, there must be one — and only one — system of record for a data element.

- **Stakeholder:** Individuals and organizations who are actively involved in the initiative, or whose interests may be positively or negatively affected as a result of execution or successful completion of the initiative.

- **Structured Data**: Data that is organized according to a predetermined structure.

- **Text Analytics**: Text analytics or text mining is the application of statistical, linguistic, and machine learning techniques on text-based data-sources to derive meaning or insight. It is the process of deriving insights from text-based content.

- **Transactional Data**: Data that relates to business events such as purchase orders and invoices.

- **Union:** The SQL UNION operator is used to combine two or more data sets with the same fields and data types. The tables that are part of the UNION should be of the same structure.

- **Unstructured Data**: Data that has no identifiable structure, such as email, social media posts, documents, audio files, images, and videos.

- **Value Stream Mapping (VSM):** VSM is a visual tool that shows the flow of process and information the company uses to produce a product or service for its customers. VSM has its origins to lean manufacturing, and the business value of VSM is to identify and remove or reduce waste in the processes, thereby increasing the efficiency in the system.

- **Visualization**: A visual abstraction of data designed for the purpose of deriving meaning or communicating information more effectively. Visuals created are often complex, but understandable, in order to convey the data.

- **Visual Analytics**: It is the science of analytical reasoning supported by visuals. In this book, concepts such as data storytelling and dashboards are associated with visual analytics.

Index

5WH framework, 37, 38
Algorithm, 86, 106, 121, 122, 188
API, 131, 177, 181
best practice, i, 22, 23, 24, 25, 32, 43, 48, 80, 119, 122, 130, 134, 140, 149, 181
Bloom's taxonomy, 38
Business Intelligence, 44, 99, 177, 181
change management, i, 24, 41, 109, 146, 148, 149, 153, 154, 159
Cross-validation, 120
dashboard, 40, 103, 112, 165, 167
Dashboard, 42, 182
Data Architecture, 128, 159, 183
data compliance, 24, 60, 91, 92, 95, 99, 100, 136, 158
data engineering, 3, 49, 50, 76, 79
Data Governance, 137, 178, 183
Data Integration, 48, 183
data lake, 49, 109, 110, 149
data lifecycle, iii, 20, 140, 150, 176
data monetization, 19, 22, 24, 124, 125, 126, 127, 128, 129, 131, 133, 134, 135
data product, 133, 134, 162, 164, 184
data quality, 75, 76, 142, 143, 175, 176

data science, 3, 50, 133, 184
data storytelling, i, 24, 145, 146, 147, 148, 149, 150, 152, 153, 154, 159
data warehouse, 49, 88, 109, 110, 149, 165, 183
database, 49, 58, 67, 68, 77, 88, 97, 112, 142, 164, 176, 181, 184, 187, 188, 189
descriptive analytics, 24, 102, 103, 104, 105, 106, 107, 110, 158, 165, 167
Digital Asset Management, 99, 177, 184
Embedded Analytics, 128, 131, 136, 159
enterprise, 36, 76, 175
Feature Engineering, 82, 85, 158, 185
Gartner, ii, 3, 6, 7, 75, 90, 101, 103, 114, 125, 134, 136, 144, 153, 181
hypothesis, 11, 38, 41, 51, 84, 185
intuition, 8, 9, 10, 11, 19, 38, 46, 85, 185
KPI, 39, 40, 42, 105, 112, 178, 186
Last Mile Analytics, 178, 186
Machine Learning, 116, 178, 186
MAD framework, 103, 104
master data, 7, 20, 59, 60, 108, 140, 142, 162, 176

Metadata, 64, 187

NPV, 152, 179

playbook, 23, 25, 173

predictive analytics, 7, 105, 115, 116, 117, 118, 124, 188

prescriptive analytics, 7, 13, 49, 106, 115, 117, 118, 119, 124, 165

questions, iii, 7, 9, 24, 28, 29, 30, 31, 32, 36, 37, 38, 39, 41, 102, 121, 123, 150, 151, 157, 162, 163, 164, 168, 171, 182

reference data, 59, 108, 140, 162

regression, 66, 86, 105, 116, 118, 121, 186

reports, 44, 61, 69, 95, 96, 102, 103, 106, 109, 110, 111, 112, 150, 165, 167

ROIC, 152

Sampling, 82, 83, 158

SoI, 131, 179, 189

SoR, 48, 131, 179, 189

SQL, 88, 109, 110, 179, 188, 189

standards, 142, 175

structured data, 58, 70

SVM, 121, 179, 188

text analytics, 70, 71

transactional data, 20, 59, 60, 68, 75, 108, 129, 162, 176, 187, 188

unstructured data, 58, 69, 70, 71, 99, 183

value, i, ii, iii, 8, 14, 15, 16, 20, 21, 22, 23, 24, 25, 27, 29, 31, 38, 42, 44, 47, 53, 62, 67, 71, 72, 74, 78, 81, 86, 90, 95, 102, 105, 106, 108, 118, 125, 128, 129, 131, 133, 134, 135, 136, 147, 151, 152, 158, 161, 162, 163, 175, 178, 184, 185, 186

visualization, 3, 7, 49, 50, 110, 146, 165, 184

WACC, 123, 152, 180

what-if scenarios, 118, 119, 122, 158

Printed in Great Britain
by Amazon